Absence of Arbitrage Valuation

Absence of Arbitrage Valuation

A Unified Framework for Pricing Assets and Securities

Paskalis Glabadanidis

palgrave
macmillan

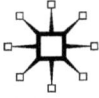

ABSENCE OF ARBITRAGE VALUATION
Copyright © Paskalis Glabadanidis, 2014.

All right reserved.

First published in 2014 by
PALGRAVE MACMILLAN®
in the United States—a division of St. Martins Press LLC,
175 Fifth Avenue, New York, NY 10010.

Where this book is distributed in the UK, Europe and the rest of the world,
his is by Palgrave Macmillan, a division of Macmillan Publishers Limited,
registered in England, company number 785998, of Houndmills,
Basingstoke, Hampshire RG21 6XS.

Palgrave Macmillan is the global academic imprint of the above companies
and has companies and representatives throughout the world.

Palgrave® and Macmillan® are registered trademarks in the United States,
the United Kingdom, Europe and other countries.

ISBN: 978–1–137–37302–1

Library of Congress Cataloging-in-Publication Data

Glabadanidis, Paskalis.
    Absence of arbitrage valuation : a unified framework for pricing assets
and securities / Paskalis Glabadanidis.
        pages cm
    Includes bibliographical references and index.
    ISBN 978–1–137–37302–1 (hardback: alk. paper)
    1. Arbitrage. 2. Securities—Valuation. 3. Investments—Valuation. I. Title.

HG4521.G5476 2014
332.64′5–dc23   2014000485

A catalogue record of the book is available from the British Library.

Design by Newgen Knowledge Works (P) Ltd., Chennai, India.

First edition: July 2014

10 9 8 7 6 5 4 3 2 1

To M. who is still learning the value of everything.

Contents

Figures

Tables

Asset Pricing Models

1.1 Future Value

Consider investing a current value of V_0 for T periods at the compound periodic rate of r. The future value of the initial investment is given simply by the following:

$$V_T = V_0(1+r)^T. \tag{1.1}$$

Note the compounding effect that follows from being able to earn interest in future periods on the interest earned in previous periods. The longer the length of the compounding period T, the more pronounced this effect will be given a fixed starting value V_0 for a fixed r. For a fixed future time period T and initial investment V_0, the compounding effect becomes much more pronounced for larger values of r.

1.2 Present Value

Consider now turning the previous question on its head and ask the following: what is the present value today at $t = 0$ equal to a given future value of V_T given a periodic opportunity cost of capital equal to r? The answer to this question can be obtained through a simple rearrangement of the future value equation in the previous section as follows:

$$V_0 = \frac{V_T}{(1+r)^T}. \tag{1.2}$$

Note that the further out into the future the cash flow is to be obtained the lower the present value, given a fixed opportunity cost.

Similarly, for a fixed future time period T, higher values for the opportunity cost r lead to lower present values today at $t = 0$.

1.3 Perpetuities

Consider an infinite sequence of cash flows of the same amount C which commences payment at $t = 1$ and never cease. This is an example of a level payment to be received in perpetuity or, more simply, a perpetuity.

The present value of all of these payments is represented by the following infinite sum:

$$V_0 = \frac{C}{1+r} + \frac{C}{(1+r)^2} + \frac{C}{(1+r)^3} + \cdots.$$

This infinite sum is an example of a geometric series and, provided that $r > 0$, converges to a finite value

$$V_0 = \frac{C}{1+r}\left(\frac{1}{1 - \left(\dfrac{1}{1+r}\right)}\right),$$

which, after some simplifications of terms in the denominator, is reduced to the following:

$$V_0 = \frac{C}{r}. \tag{1.3}$$

Another useful sequence of cash flows is a growing perpetuity. This is very similar to the example just considered where the first cash flow C takes place again at $t = 1$ and is paid forever, but this time every subsequent payment increases at the rate of g. The present value of this growing perpetuity is given by the infinite sequence:

$$V_0 = \frac{C}{(1+r)} + \frac{C(1+g)}{(1+r)^2} + \frac{C(1+g)^2}{(1+r)^3} + \cdots.$$

This is yet another example of an infinite sum of a geometric series which converges to a finite value, provided that $g < r$, as follows:

$$V_0 = \frac{C}{(1+r)}\left(\frac{1}{1 - \left(\dfrac{1+g}{1+r}\right)}\right),$$

which, after some simplifications, leads to the following:

$$V_0 = \frac{C}{r-g}. \tag{1.4}$$

Note that if $g \geq r$, then the present value of the growing perpetuity is infinite. The above formula is only valid for the case where the growth rate is less than r. Applying the formula to a case where $g \geq r$ is a mistake as witnessed by the resulting negative present value.

1.4   Annuities

Let us now consider a finite stream of cash flows which starts at $t = 1$ and lasts until $t = T > 1$ where the same periodic payment C is being paid in every period. The present value of this level annuity is given by

$$V_0 = \frac{C}{(1+r)} + \frac{C}{(1+r)^2} + \cdots + \frac{C}{(1+r)^T}.$$

We can evaluate this finite geometric series directly or, alternatively, we realize that the level annuity can be represented as the difference between two perpetuities. The first perpetuity pays off C in every period starting with $t = 1$, while the second perpetuity pays off C in every period starting with $t = T + 1$. The difference between the payoffs of these two perpetuities comprises the payoffs of the level annuity. Hence, the present values of the level annuity is the difference between the present values of the two perpetuities:

$$V_0 = \frac{C}{r} - \frac{C}{r}\left(\frac{1}{(1+r)^T}\right),$$

which, after collecting terms, reduces to

$$V_0 = \frac{C}{r}\left[1 - \frac{1}{(1+r)^T}\right]. \tag{1.5}$$

Next, let us consider a more general annuity where the period payment increases in every period at the rate of g where the initial payment C takes place again at $t = 1$ and the last payment is at $t = T > 1$. The present value of this growing annuity is equal to

$$V_0 = \frac{C}{(1+r)} + \frac{C(1+g)}{(1+r)^2} + \cdots + \frac{C(1+g)^{T-1}}{(1+r)^T}.$$

We can evaluate this finite sum using the geometric series formula or, alternatively, we can realize that the payoffs of the growing annuity can be represented as the difference between the payoffs of two growing perpetuities. The first growing perpetuity starts at $t = 1$ with an initial payment of C while the second growing perpetuity starts at $t = T + 1$ with an initial payment of $C(1 + g)^T$. Both perpetual payments grow at the rate of g per period. The difference between their present values at $t = 0$ is given by

$$V_0 = \frac{C}{r - g} - \frac{C(1 + g)^T}{r - g} \left(\frac{1}{(1 + r)^T} \right),$$

which, after collecting terms, yields

$$V_0 = \frac{C}{r - g} \left[1 - \frac{(1 + g)^T}{(1 + r)^T} \right]. \tag{1.6}$$

Note that in this case there are a finite number of terms, so we can have $g > r$ and arrive at the appropriate positive present value of the growing annuity.

1.5   Capital Asset Pricing Model

1.5.1   The Case of Two Risky Securities

Suppose that the excess return of asset A is given by $\mu_A = E(r_A) - r_f$ and the excess return of asset B is $\mu_B = E(r_B) - r_f$. Let the standard deviation of A's excess return be σ_A and the standard deviation of B's excess return be σ_B. Finally, let the correlation between A's and B's excess returns be given by ρ_{AB}. Consider the problem of finding the tangent portfolio which is fully invested in a combination of both assets and has the highest ratio of excess return per unit standard deviation (the Sharpe ratio). The solution to this problem is

$$w_{tg,A} = \frac{\mu_A \sigma_B^2 - \mu_B \rho_{AB} \sigma_A \sigma_B}{\mu_A \sigma_B^2 + \mu_B \sigma_A^2 - (\mu_A + \mu_B) \rho_{AB} \sigma_A \sigma_B}, \tag{1.7}$$

$$w_{tg,B} = \frac{\mu_B \sigma_A^2 - \mu_A \rho_{AB} \sigma_A \sigma_B}{\mu_A \sigma_B^2 + \mu_B \sigma_A^2 - (\mu_A + \mu_B) \rho_{AB} \sigma_A \sigma_B}. \tag{1.8}$$

Two special cases are worth investigating a bit further. Suppose, at first, that $\rho_{AB} = -1$. Then the resulting portfolio is riskless and, hence, it has to have a zero-expected excess return in order to prevent an arbitrage opportunity which leads to the following restriction:

$$\mu_A \sigma_B + \mu_B \sigma_A = 0, \tag{1.9}$$

$$s_A = -s_B, \tag{1.10}$$

where $s_A = \mu_A/\sigma_A$ is the Sharpe ratio of security A and $s_B = \mu_B/\sigma_B$ is the Sharpe ratio of security B. What this means is that two securities with perfectly negatively correlated returns have to lie on two rays from the origin in excess return–standard deviation space that are symmetrical around the horizontal axis. Any other possibility will lead to an arbitrage opportunity.

The other extreme case that results in a riskless portfolio is the case of $\rho_{AB} = +1$. In this case, we also require that this portfolio has a zero excess return which leads to the following condition:

$$\mu_A \sigma_B - \mu_B \sigma_A = 0, \tag{1.11}$$

$$s_A = s_B. \tag{1.12}$$

In this case, two securities with perfectly positively correlated excess returns have to have the same Sharpe ratio or lie on the same ray from the origin in excess return–standard deviation space. Any other possibility will lead to an arbitrage opportunity.

Similar to the tangent portfolio, we can define the global minimum variance portfolio as the one that is fully invested in a combination of both securities such that the variance of the portfolio return is as low as possible. The optimal minimum variance portfolio weights are given as follows:

$$w_{mv,A} = \frac{\sigma_B^2 - \rho_{AB}\sigma_A\sigma_B}{\sigma_A^2 + \sigma_B^2 - 2\rho_{AB}\sigma_A\sigma_B}, \tag{1.13}$$

$$w_{mv,B} = \frac{\sigma_A^2 - \rho_{AB}\sigma_A\sigma_B}{\sigma_A^2 + \sigma_B^2 - 2\rho_{AB}\sigma_A\sigma_B}. \tag{1.14}$$

Again, two special cases and their consequences are worth noting. First, consider the case of $\rho_{AB} = -1$. The minimum variance portfolio weights simplify to

$$w_{mv,A} = \frac{\sigma_B}{\sigma_A + \sigma_B}, \tag{1.15}$$

$$w_{mv,B} = \frac{\sigma_A}{\sigma_A + \sigma_B}. \tag{1.16}$$

It is straightforward to verify that the variance of return of the minimum variance portfolio in this case is zero. In order to avoid an arbitrage opportunity, the excess return of the minimum variance portfolio in this special case better be equal to zero which leads to the following constraint:

$$\mu_A \sigma_B + \mu_B \sigma_A = 0, \tag{1.17}$$

$$s_A = -s_B. \tag{1.18}$$

In other words, two assets with perfectly negatively correlated excess returns have to lie on two rays from the origin in excess return–standard deviation space symmetric around the horizontal axis. Any other possibility will lead to an arbitrage possibility.

Consider next the case of $\rho_{AB} = +1$. In this case, the minimum variance portfolio weights simplify to the following:

$$w_{mv,A} = \frac{\sigma_B}{\sigma_B - \sigma_A}, \tag{1.19}$$

$$w_{mv,B} = \frac{-\sigma_A}{\sigma_B - \sigma_A}. \tag{1.20}$$

This portfolio also has a zero return variance and is, in effect, riskless. Hence, in order to avoid an arbitrage opportunity it has to have an excess return of zero which leads to the following:

$$\mu_A \sigma_B - \mu_B \sigma_A = 0, \tag{1.21}$$

$$s_A = s_B, \tag{1.22}$$

or the Sharpe ratios of both securities have to be equal to each other. Hence, two securities with perfectly positively correlated returns have to lie on the same ray from the origin in excess return-standard deviation space. If the two securities with perfectly positively correlated returns had different Sharpe ratios, then it would lead to an arbitrage opportunity.

1.5.2 The Case of Multiple Risky Securities

In the general case of N risky securities, let us define a mean vector of the expected excess returns, μ, as well as a variance–covariance matrix of excess returns, Σ. In this case, the tangent portfolio weights are given by

$$w_{tg} = \frac{\Sigma^{-1} \mu}{1_N' \Sigma^{-1} \mu}, \tag{1.23}$$

where 1_N is a column vector of ones. The expected excess return of the tangent portfolio is equal to

$$\mu_{tg} = \frac{\mu'\Sigma^{-1}\mu}{1_N'\Sigma^{-1}\mu}. \tag{1.24}$$

The variance of the excess return of the tangent portfolio is equal to

$$\sigma_{tg}^2 = \frac{\mu'\Sigma^{-1}\mu}{(1_N'\Sigma^{-1}\mu)^2}, \tag{1.25}$$

while the Sharpe ratio of the tangent portfolio is

$$s_{tg} = \sqrt{\mu'\Sigma^{-1}\mu}. \tag{1.26}$$

Next, let us define the risky securities beta vector, β, as the ratio of the covariance between the excess returns of the risky securities and the excess return of the tangent portfolio and the excess return variance of the tangent portfolio. Straightforward linear algebraic arguments lead to the following value for the β vector:

$$\beta = \mu\frac{1_N'\Sigma^{-1}\mu}{\mu'\Sigma^{-1}\mu}. \tag{1.27}$$

Note that we can use our knowledge about the excess return of the tangent portfolio to rewrite the previous equation as follows:

$$\beta = \frac{\mu}{\mu_{tg}}. \tag{1.28}$$

Rearranging the terms, above equation leads to the of Sharpe (1964):

$$\mu = \beta\mu_{tg}, \tag{1.29}$$

$$E(r_i) - r_f = \beta_i\left[E(r_{tg}) - r_f\right]. \tag{1.30}$$

Similarly, we can obtain the global minimum variance portfolio weights as follows:

$$w_{mv} = \frac{\Sigma^{-1}1_N}{1_N'\Sigma^{-1}1_N}. \tag{1.31}$$

The expected excess return of the minimum variance portfolio is equal to

$$\mu_{mv} = \frac{\mu'\Sigma^{-1}1_N}{1_N'\Sigma^{-1}1_N}, \tag{1.32}$$

the excess return variance of the minimum variance portfolio is given by

$$\sigma_{mv}^2 = \frac{1}{1_N' \Sigma^{-1} 1_N}, \tag{1.33}$$

and the Sharpe ratio of the minimum variance portfolio is

$$s_{mv} = \frac{\mu' \Sigma^{-1} 1_N}{\sqrt{1_N' \Sigma^{-1} 1_N}}. \tag{1.34}$$

A few relations between the moments of the minimum variance and the tangent portfolio are of independent interest. First, it is possible to show that the excess return per unit return variance is the same for both the minimum variance portfolio and the tangent portfolio or

$$\frac{\mu_{tg}}{\sigma_{tg}^2} = \frac{\mu_{mv}}{\sigma_{mv}^2}. \tag{1.35}$$

Secondly, the correlation between the excess return of security i and the excess return of the tangent portfolio is equal to the ratio of the i-th security's Sharpe ratio and the tangent portfolio's Sharpe ratio:

$$\rho_{i,tg} = \frac{s_i}{s_{tg}}. \tag{1.36}$$

Thirdly, the idiosyncratic return variance of security i is given by

$$\sigma_{\epsilon_i}^2 = \sigma_i^2 \left(1 - \frac{s_i^2}{s_{tg}^2}\right). \tag{1.37}$$

Fourth, the beta of the minimum variance portfolio with the tangent portfolio is positive but strictly less than one and is given by

$$\beta_{mv,tg} = \frac{\sigma_{mv}^2}{\sigma_{tg}^2}. \tag{1.38}$$

Finally, the correlation between the excess return of the minimum variance portfolio and the excess return of the tangent portfolio is also positive and less than 1 and is equal to

$$\rho_{mv,tg} = \frac{\sigma_{mv}}{\sigma_{tg}}. \tag{1.39}$$

1.6   Fama–French Three-Factor Model

The following model was proposed by Fama and French (1992):

$$E(R_i) = R_f + \beta_i(E(R_m) - R_f) + s_i\text{SMB} + h_i\text{HML}, \tag{1.40}$$

where the additional variable s_i is the standardized covariance between asset i and portfolio small minus big (SMB) and h_i is the standardized covariance between asset i and portfolio high minus low (HML). Portfolio SMB consists of long positions in small-cap stocks and short positions in large-cap stocks while portfolio HML consists of long positions in value stocks (high book-to-market ratios) and short positions in growth stocks (low book-to-market ratios).

The excess value–weighted return on all CRSP firms incorporated in the United States and listed on NYSE, AMEX, or NASDAQ is denoted by MKT. The description of the construction of the size, value, and momentum factors are as follows. The six portfolios used to construct the size and value factors are based on a double sort of all NYSE, AMEX, and NASDAQ stocks with available market capitalization and book value of equity based on size and the book-to-market ratio. The 50th percentile is used to separate small-cap from large-cap stocks while the top 70th percentile of the book-to-market ratio is used to separate value from value-neutral stocks and the bottom 30th percentile of the book-to-market ratio is the cutoff between growth and value-neutral stocks.

Small value (SV)	Big value (BV)
Small neutral (SN)	Big neutral (BN)
Small growth (SG)	Big growth (BG)

The value-weighted return of the small-cap factor SMB is calculated as the difference between the equal-weighted small-cap portfolio returns across the value spectrum and the equal-weighted large-cap portfolio returns for value, growth, and value-neutral stocks as follows:

$$\text{SMB} = \tfrac{1}{3}(\text{SV} + \text{SN} + \text{SG}) - \tfrac{1}{3}(\text{BV} + \text{BN} + \text{BG}). \tag{1.41}$$

The value-weighted return of the value factor HML is given by the difference between the value-weighted returns of the high book-to-market stocks across market caps and the value-weighted returns of the low book-to-market small-cap and large-cap stocks as follows:

$$HML = \tfrac{1}{2}(SV + BV) - \tfrac{1}{2}(SG + BG). \tag{1.42}$$

1.7 Carhart Four-Factor Model

In his work on mutual fund performance, Carhart (1997) proposed the following extension to the Fama–French three-factor model:

$$E(R_i) = R_f + \beta_i(E(R_m) - R_f) + s_i SMB + h_i HML + p_i WML, \tag{1.43}$$

where the additional variable p_i is the standardized covariance between asset i and portfolio winners minus losers (WML). Portfolio WML consists of long positions in stocks that have increased significantly in value over the course of the past year (winners) and short positions in stocks that have decreased significantly in value during the past year (losers).

The six portfolios used to construct the momentum factor are based on the following double sort of all NYSE, AMEX, and NASDAQ stocks with available prior monthly returns based on market capitalization using the 50th percentile as the cutoff point between small cap and large cap as well as prior 12-month return using the top 70th percentile to separate past winners from medium performing stocks and the bottom 30th percentile to distinguish losing stocks from medium past performers.

Small up (SU)	Big up (BU)
Small medium (SM)	Big medium (BM)
Small down (SD)	Big down (BD)

Value-weighted momentum portfolio returns UMD are calculated based on the spread between the value-weighted return of past winners and the value-weighted return of past losers as follows:

$$UMD = \tfrac{1}{2}(SU + BU) - \tfrac{1}{2}(SD + BD). \tag{1.44}$$

1.8 Arbitrage Pricing Theory

The previous two multifactor models are primarily driven by empirical regularities discovered in the data rather than rigorous theoretical work. One of the first theoretically motivated asset pricing models was proposed in Ross (1976). The model is agnostic about the nature and identity of the pervasive sources of systematic risk but does assume that there are K separate risk factors that drive asset returns as follows:

$$\tilde{R}_i = E(R_i) + \beta_{i,1}\tilde{F}_1 + \beta_{i,2}\tilde{F}_2 + \cdots + \beta_{i,K}\tilde{F}_K + \tilde{\epsilon}_i, \tag{1.45}$$

where $\beta_{i,1}, \beta_{i,2}, \ldots, \beta_{i,K}$ are the standardized covariances between asset i and each of the K factors, $\tilde{F}_1, \tilde{F}_2, \ldots, \tilde{F}_K$ are the factor returns, and $\tilde{\epsilon}_i$ are the idiosyncratic security innovations.

Through the construction of asymptotically well-diversified portfolios, one can eliminate all idiosyncratic risk and can show that the expected asset returns are proportional to asset exposures to risk factors (betas) and factor risk premia:

$$E(R_i) = R_f + \beta_{i,1}E(F_1) + \beta_{i,2}E(F_2) + \cdots + \beta_{i,K}E(F_K), \tag{1.46}$$

where $E(F_1), E(F_2), \ldots, E(F_K)$ are the risk premia on factors $1, 2, \ldots, K$. The factors $1, 2, \ldots, K$ are estimated statistically based on how asset prices covary with each other using factor analysis or principal components decomposition of the entire variance–covariance matrix of asset returns.

A sketch of the proof is based on a cross-sectional projection argument. Suppose we know the true vector of securities' expected returns $E(R)$ and the factor loading matrix B as well as the variance–covariance matrix of idiosyncratic returns Ω. Projecting the vector of expected returns on B obliquely along Ω is equivalent to a generalized least squares regression with an intercept equal to the zero-beta return and slopes equal to the respective factor risk premia, $E(F_k)$. Take the fitted residuals, $\hat{e}$, from this cross-sectional regression and construct an arbitrage portfolio as $w = \hat{e}/(\hat{e}'\hat{e})$. By construction, we have that the portfolio weights sum up to zero and they have zero loadings on any of the risk factors. Similarly, by bounding the largest eigenvalue of Ω we can show that the variance of the arbitrage portfolio is proportional to $1/(\hat{e}'\hat{e})$ for a fixed number of securities. Letting the number of securities increase without bound leads to a vanishing portfolio risk in the limit. Hence, in order to avoid such a limiting arbitrage opportunity, the vector of securities' expected returns has to be proportional to their respective factor loadings as in the arbitrage pricing theory (APT) equation above.[1]

1.9   Macroeconomic Multifactor Models

Chen, Roll, and Ross (1986) present a multifactor model that is in part motivated by trying to identify the pervasive sources of risk that drive asset returns using macroeconomic state variables:

$$E(R_i) = R_f + \beta_{i,1}E(F_1) + \beta_{i,2}E(F_2) + \cdots + \beta_{i,K}E(F_K), \qquad (1.47)$$

where the difference between APT and macro multifactor models is that in the APT the factors are estimated statistically while in this model the factors are prespecified. The most commonly used state variables include real gross domestic product (GDP) growth, an index of industrial production, the unexpected inflation rate, and the term structure spread (long-term minus short-term interest rates).

Problems

1. Consider a sequence of cash flows with a starting value of 1,000 next year, growing annually at the rate of 5% per year for the next 40 years. Suppose the opportunity cost of capital is 4%. Find the present value today of this growing annuity. What is the future value of this growing annuity at the end of 40 years from today? What assumption is necessary to answer the previous question?

2. Find the arbitrage in each of the following combinations for securities' excess expected returns, return variances, and correlations:

   (a) $\mu_A = 0.1$, $\mu_B = 0.2$, $\rho_{AB} = -1$, $\sigma_A = 0.2$, $\sigma_B = 0.4$.
   (b) $\mu_A = 0.1$, $\mu_B = 0.16$, $\rho_{AB} = 1$, $\sigma_A = 0.2$, $\sigma_B = 0.3$.
   (c) $\mu_A = 0.1$, $\mu_B = -0.1$, $\rho_{AB} = -1$, $\sigma_A = 0.2$, $\sigma_B = 0.3$.

3. Consider a world with only two risky securities. Security A has an expected excess return of $\mu_A = 0.05$ and return standard deviation of $\sigma_A = 0.5$. Security B has an expected excess return of $\mu_B = 0.10$ and return standard deviation of $\sigma_B = 0.5$. The correlation between the two securities' returns is $\rho_{AB} = 0.2$. What are the compositions of the minimum variance and tangent portfolios? What are the betas of each of the two securities with the market portfolio and what are their idiosyncratic return standard deviations equal to? Verify that the expected excess returns of each security are proportional to their respective betas and the excess return on the market portfolio.

4. Consider a world with three securities. The returns on all three securities is driven by one latent factor with unit factor return variance and zero mean. The vector of expected returns is given by $E(R) = [0.10, 0.12, 0.14]'$ and the vector of securities' loadings on the latent factor is given by $b = [1, 1.2, 1.5]'$. Find the zero-beta return and the latent factor risk premium. Construct a portfolio that has no exposure to the latent factor and 100% expected return. Is this an arbitrage? What would be the consequences of trading this portfolio on the securities' expected returns?

2

Discounted Cash Flow Valuation

2.1 Dividend Growth Models

2.1.1 Single-Stage Models

The simplest version of the dividend discount model is most applicable to mature companies with stable earnings and dividends growing at relatively low rates in line with the growth in aggregate economic output. In this case, we can apply the growing perpetuity formula to the dividend per share, DPS_0, forecast to grow at the rate of g in perpetuity with r_e as the required rate of return on equity. This leads to the following intrinsic value per share:

$$V_0^E = \frac{DPS_0(1+g)}{r_e - g} \tag{2.1}$$

Figure 2.1 depicts the forecasted growth rate of dividend per share as a function of time in a single-stage dividend discount model.

A version of this model sometimes starts with next periods expected DPS_1, in which case the above expression simplifies even further to

$$V_0^E = \frac{DPS_1}{r_e - g}. \tag{2.2}$$

2.1.2 Two-Stage Models

It is usually difficult to apply a one-stage discounted cash flow (DCF) model in the case of firms that are expected to have dividends grow at higher than normal growth rates at least for some time. To this purpose, it is natural to extend the assumption behind the growth rate forecasts to include two stages. The first stage that only lasts for a

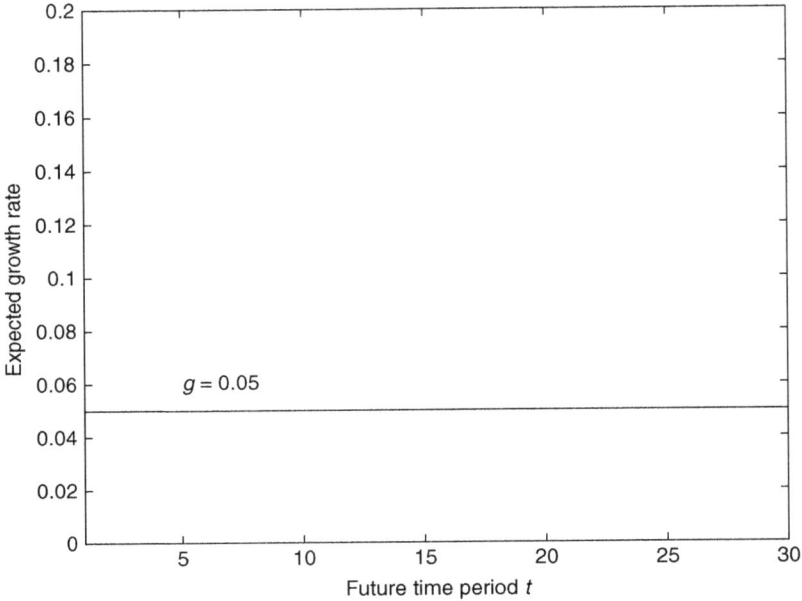

Figure 2.1   Future forecasts of the expected growth rate in a single-stage DCF model.

number of periods, n, will typically have a higher growth rate, g_1, while the second stage will have a lower growth rate of g_2, perhaps no higher than the nominal growth rate of aggregate economic output that lasts forever. Both stages can potentially have different required rates of return on equity $r_{e,1}$ and $r_{e,2}$, respectively. Combining the growing annuity formula with the growing perpetuity formula from the previous chapter, we obtain the following expression for the present intrinsic value at $t = 0$:

$$
V_0^E = \frac{\mathrm{DPS}_0(1+g_1)\left(1 - \left(\dfrac{1+g_1}{1+r_{e,1}}\right)^n\right)}{r_{e,1} - g_1} + \frac{V_n^E}{(1+r_{e,1})^n}, \tag{2.3}
$$

where V_n^E is the terminal value at date n given by

$$
V_n^E = \frac{\mathrm{DPS}_{n+1}}{r_{e,2} - g_2} = \frac{\mathrm{DPS}_0(1+g_1)^n(1+g_2)}{r_{e,2} - g_2}. \tag{2.4}
$$

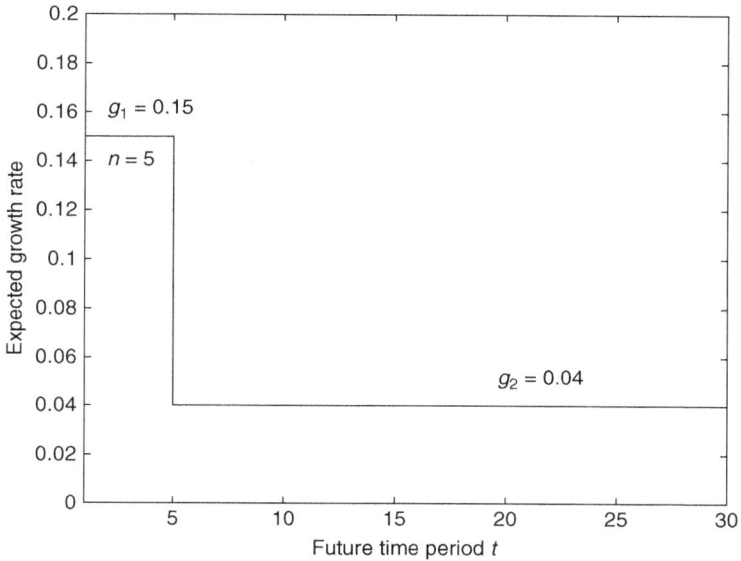

Figure 2.2 Future forecasts of the expected growth rate in a two-stage DCF model.

Combining the previous two equations leads to a more compact albeit less intuitive expression for the present value of all future dividends in the simple two-stage model as follows:

$$V_0^E = \frac{\mathrm{DPS}_0(1+g_1)\left(1 - \left(\dfrac{1+g_1}{1+r_{e,1}}\right)^n\right)}{r_{e,1} - g_1}$$
$$+ \frac{\mathrm{DPS}_0(1+g_1)^n(1+g_2)}{(r_{e,2} - g_2)(1+r_{e,1})^n}. \tag{2.5}$$

Figure 2.2 portrays the forecasted growth rate of dividend per share as a function of time in a two-stage dividend discount model.

Note that the above two-stage DCF model involves a discontinuity in the growth rate of dividends, i.e., there is an abrupt change at $t = n$ from g_1 to g_2. One way to correct for this is to assume that the growth rate of dividends will change linearly, i.e., gradually, over a certain period of time between the two growth rates. Such a model exists and is referred to as the H model after the original notation in the article that derived and proposed this idea. Assuming that the initial growth rate in dividends per share is g_1 and that it will change linearly over

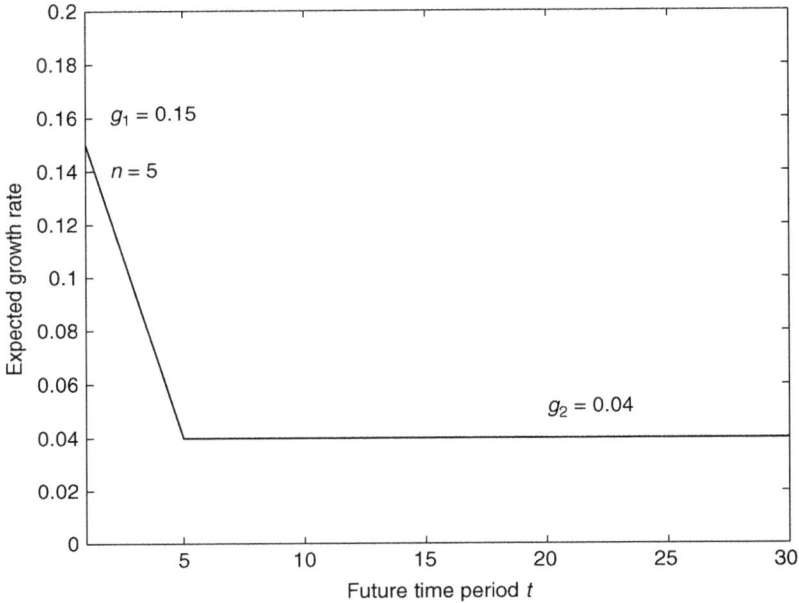

Figure 2.3   Future forecasts of the expected growth rate in the H model.

the next n periods to g_2 and stay at g_2 forever, the present intrinsic value per share is as follows:

$$V_0^E = \frac{DPS_0(1 + g_2 + (n/2)(g_1 - g_2))}{r_e - g_2} \tag{2.6}$$

Figure 2.3 presents the forecasted growth rate of dividends per share over time in the H model.

Note that in the H model the required rate of return on equity is the same in both stages, which can sometimes be a disadvantage if the forecasts call for different levels of systematic risk in each stage.

2.1.3   Three-Stage Models

Consider next the following set of forecasts for future dividends per share. Initially, they grow for n_1 periods at the rate of g_1 which attracts a required rate of return on equity of $r_{e,1}$. Next, the growth rate in dividends per share is forecast to change linearly from g_1 to g_2 over the course of n_2 periods. Finally, this is followed by a perpetual stage of stable growth at the rate of g_2. The transition stage and the stable stage both attract a required rate of return on equity of $r_{e,2}$. This model is sometimes referred to as the E model. This gives a terminal value at date n_1 given by

$$V_{n_1}^E = \frac{\mathrm{DPS}_0(1+g_1)^{n_1}(1+g_2+(n_2/2)(g_1-g_2))}{(r_{e,2}-g_2)}. \tag{2.7}$$

Combining this terminal value from H model with the first stage of high growth leads to the following expression for the value per share in the three-stage model:

$$V_0^E = \frac{\mathrm{DPS}_0(1+g_1)\left(1-\left(\dfrac{1+g_1}{1+r_{e,1}}\right)^{n_1}\right)}{r_{e,1}-g_1}$$
$$+ \frac{\mathrm{DPS}_0(1+g_1)^{n_1}(1+g_2+(n_2/2)(g_1-g_2))}{(r_{e,2}-g_2)(1+r_{e,1})^{n_1}}. \tag{2.8}$$

Figure 2.4 plots the forecasted growth rate of dividends per share over time in a three-stage dividend discount model where the second and the third stage use the H model.

Occasionally, one might want to have three stages with distinctly different but constant dividend growth rates for the duration of each stage. Consider a model where initially dividends per share are expected to grow at the rate of g_1 for n_1 periods, then at the rate of g_2 for n_2 periods, and finally at the rate of g_3 forever. It is straightforward to show that the present intrinsic value per share in such a three-stage DCF model is

$$V_0^E = \frac{\mathrm{DPS}_0(1+g_1)\left(1-\left(\dfrac{1+g_1}{1+r_{e,1}}\right)^{n_1}\right)}{r_{e,1}-g_1}$$
$$+ \frac{V_{n_1}^E}{(1+r_{e,1})^{n_1}} + \frac{V_{n_1+n_2}^E}{(1+r_{e,1})^{n_1}(1+r_{e,2})^{n_2}}, \tag{2.9}$$

Figure 2.5 plots the forecasted growth rate of dividend per share over time in a three-stage dividend discount model where each stage has its own distinct growth rate.

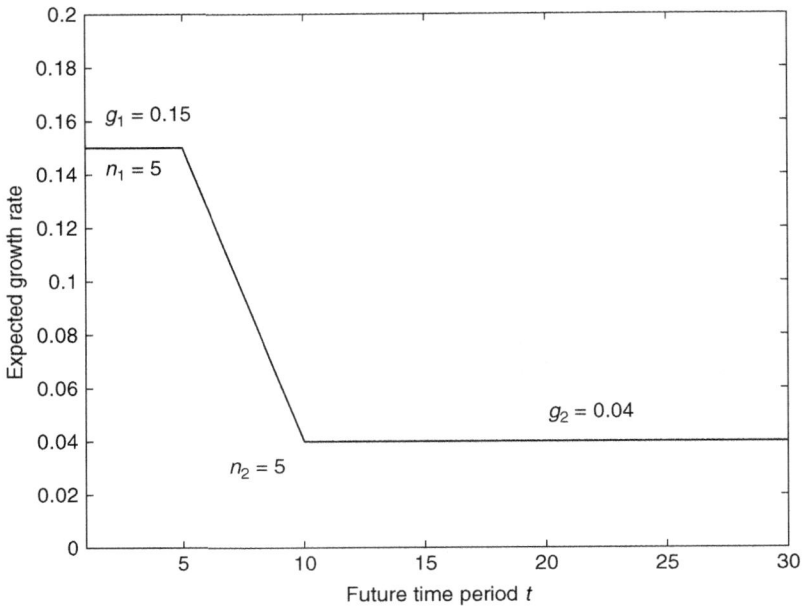

Figure 2.4   Future forecasts of the expected growth rate in the E model.

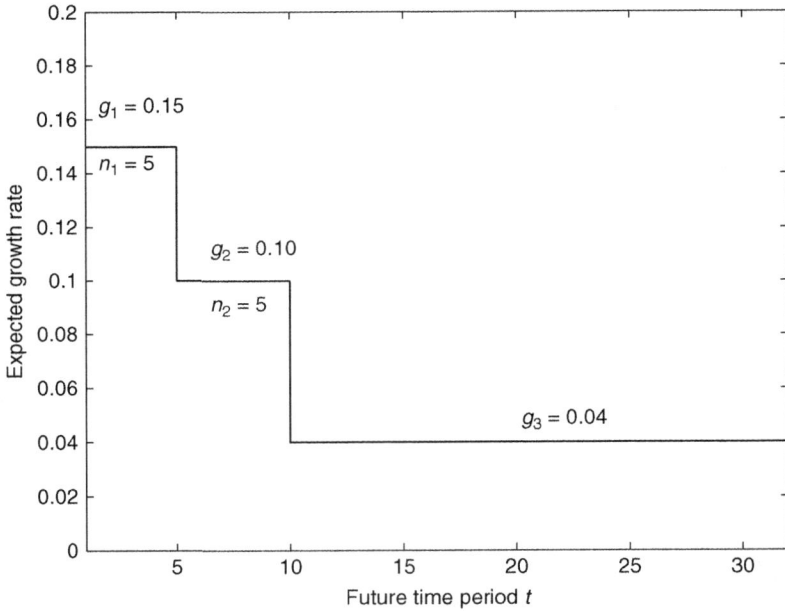

Figure 2.5   Future forecasts of the expected growth rate in a three-stage DCF model.

where

$$V^E_{n_1} = \frac{DPS_0(1+g_1)^{n_1}(1+g_2)\left(1-\left(\frac{1+g_2}{1+r_{e,2}}\right)^{n_2}\right)}{r_{e,2}-g_2},$$

$$V^E_{n_1+n_2} = \frac{DPS_0(1+g_1)^{n_1}(1+g_2)^{n_2}(1+g_3)}{r_{e,3}-g_3}$$

are the present value at $t=0$ of the third-stage dividends per share and the present value at $t=0$ of the second-stage dividends per share, respectively.

2.2   Equity Free-Cash Flow

The free cash flow to equity is defined as the cash flow left for disbursement to shareholders after all the company's reinvestment needs into additional long- and short-term assets have been met. The concept also makes adjustments for some noncash expenses that are recognized as legitimate expenses for the purposes of assessing corporate income tax, like depreciation for example. The technical definition of the equity-free cash flow is

$$FCFE = NI + Depreciation - CapEx - \Delta WC + \Delta Debt, \qquad (2.10)$$
$$= NI - (CapEx - Depreciation) - \Delta WC + \Delta Debt, \qquad (2.11)$$

where NI is the net after-tax income, CapEx is the total capital expenditure, WC is the net working capital, and ΔX stands for the change in variable X. Sometimes, it is more frugal to refer to CapEx − Depreciation as the net capital expenditure. The formula clearly takes into account the fact that depreciation is not a cash expense and that only the net capital expenditure, over and above any depreciation charges is what matters for the purposes of determining any remaining equity-free cash flows. Similarly, the change in the indebtedness of the firm is a potential source of cash flow to shareholders as new net debt issues are available to shareholders as both a source of investment and/or a source of cash to pay dividends to or buy back shares from shareholders.

2.2.1   Single-Stage FCFE Model

The value of the equity in a firm in the DCF framework with a single stage of perpetual growth is given by the present value of all future firm cash flows discounted at the required rate of return on equity:

$$V_0^E = \frac{FCFE_0(1+g)}{r_e - g},$$ (2.12)

where V_0^E is the intrinsic value of equity at $t = 0$, $FCFE_0$ is current free cash flow to equity at $t = 0$, r_e is the cost of equity, and g is the perpetual FCFE growth rate.

2.2.2   Two-Stage FCFE Model

When more flexible forecasts are needed in equity-free cash flow valuation, it makes sense to use two stages with separate growth rates, required rates of return on equity, and reinvestment rates. A straightforward application of all the DCF models in the previous section apply here as well. Suppose that we are forecasting free cash flow to the firm to grow initially at the rate of $g_1 = b_1 \times ROE_1$ for n periods. Thereafter, the free cash flow to equity is expected to grow at the rate of $g_2 = b_2 \times ROE_2$ in perpetuity. If the initial free cash flow to equity per share is $FCFE_0$ and the respective required rates of return on equity in the two stages are $r_{e,1}$ and $r_{e,2}$, then the intrinsic equity value per share is given by

$$V_0^E = \frac{FCFE_0(1+g_1)\left[1 - \left(\frac{1+g_1}{1+r_{e,1}}\right)^n\right]}{r_{e,1} - g_1}$$
$$+ \frac{FCFE_0(1+g_1)^n(1+g_2)}{(r_{e,2} - g_2)(1+r_{e,1})^n}.$$ (2.13)

Note that the first stage is just a growing annuity and, hence, we can have an arbitrarily large g_1 relative to $r_{e,1}$. The second stage is a growing perpetuity, so we have to be careful to avoid infinite intrinsic values by making sure that our forecast for g_2 is strictly less than $r_{e,2}$.[1]

A simpler two-stage FCFE model arises if we are willing to forego the generality of having two separate required rates of return on equity and insist on a continuous change in the FCFE growth rate. Adapting the H model to the case of FCFE leads to following straightforward expression:

$$V_0^E = \frac{FCFE_0(1 + g_2 + (n/2)(g_1 - g_2))}{r_e - g_2}.$$ (2.14)

2.2.3 Three-Stage FCFE Model

Consider next the following set of forecasts for future dividends per share. Initially, they grow for n_1 periods at the rate of g_1 which attracts a required rate of return on equity of $r_{e,1}$. Next, the growth rate in dividends per share is forecast to change linearly from g_1 to g_2 over the course of n_2 periods. Finally, this is followed by a perpetual stage of stable growth at the rate of g_2. The transition stage and the stable stage both attract a required rate of return on equity of $r_{e,2}$. This gives a terminal value at date n_1 given by

$$V_{n_1}^E = \frac{\text{FCFE}_0(1+g_1)^{n_1}(1+g_2+(n_2/2)(g_1-g_2))}{(r_{e,2}-g_2)}. \tag{2.15}$$

Combining this terminal value from H model with the first stage of high growth leads to the following expression for the value per share in the three-stage model:

$$V_0^E = \frac{\text{FCFE}_0(1+g_1)\left(1-\left(\frac{1+g_1}{1+r_{e,1}}\right)^{n_1}\right)}{r_{e,1}-g_1}$$
$$+ \frac{\text{FCFE}_0(1+g_1)^{n_1}(1+g_2+(n_2/2)(g_1-g_2))}{(r_{e,2}-g_2)(1+r_{e,1})^{n_1}}. \tag{2.16}$$

Occasionally, one might want to have three stages with distinctly different but constant dividend growth rates for the duration of each stage. Consider a model where initially dividends per share are expected to grow at the rate of g_1 for n_1 periods, then at the rate of g_2 for n_2 periods, and finally at the rate of g_3 forever. It is straightforward to show that the present intrinsic value per share in such a three-stage FCFE model is

$$V_0^E = \frac{\text{FCFE}_0(1+g_1)\left(1-\left(\frac{1+g_1}{1+r_{e,1}}\right)^{n_1}\right)}{r_{e,1}-g_1}$$
$$+ \frac{V_{n_1}^E}{(1+r_{e,1})^{n_1}} + \frac{V_{n_1+n_2}^E}{(1+r_{e,1})^{n_1}(1+r_{e,2})^{n_2}}, \tag{2.17}$$

where

$$V_{n_1}^E = \frac{\text{FCFE}_0(1+g_1)^{n_1}(1+g_2)\left(1-\left(\frac{1+g_2}{1+r_{e,2}}\right)^{n_2}\right)}{r_{e,2}-g_2},$$

$$V^E_{n_1+n_2} = \frac{FCFE_0(1+g_1)^{n_1}(1+g_2)^{n_2}(1+g_3)}{r_{e,3}-g_3}$$

are the present value at $t = 0$ of the third-stage FCFE and the present value at $t = 0$ of the second-stage FCFE, respectively.

2.3   Firm Free Cash Flow

The free cash flow to the firm is defined as the cash flow left for disbursement to both shareholders and bondholders after all the company's reinvestment needs into additional long- and short-term assets have been met. Similar to the equity-free cash flow, we need to make adjustments for some noncash expenses that are recognized as legitimate expenses for the purposes of assessing corporate income tax, like depreciation. The technical definition of the firm free cash flow is

$$FCFF = EBIT \times (1 - T_c) + Depreciation - CapEx - \Delta WC, \quad (2.18)$$

$$= EBIT \times (1 - T_c) - (CapEx - Depreciation) - \Delta WC, \quad (2.19)$$

where EBIT is the net after-tax income, CapEx is the total capital expenditure, WC is the net working capital, and ΔX stands for the change in variable X. Occasionally, we refer to $CapEx - Depreciation$ as the net capital expenditure. The formula clearly takes into account the fact that depreciation is not a cash expense and that only the net capital expenditure, over and above any depreciation charges, is what matters for the purposes of determining any remaining equity-free cash flows. Note that since we are defining the firm free cash as available to both shareholders and bondholders, we can no longer count any additional borrowing as a source of additional cash flow to the firm because they would come from existing or new bondholders. The other notable difference between FCFF and FCFE is the difference between net income, NI, and after-tax earnings before interest, $EBIT(1 - T_c)$. The link between these two is driven by the after-tax interest expense, $IntExp(1 - T_c)$, as follows:

$$EBIT(1 - T_c) = NI + IntExp(1 - T_c). \quad (2.20)$$

2.3.1   Single-Stage FCFF Model

The value of the firm in the DCF framework with a single stage of perpetual growth is just the present value of all future firm cash flows discounted at the firm weighted average cost of capital:

$$V_0 = \frac{\text{FCFF}_0(1+g)}{\text{WACC} - g},$$ (2.21)

where FCFF_0 is the expected free cash flow to the firm next year, g is the expected perpetual FCFF growth rate, and WACC is the weighted average cost of capital given by

$$\text{WACC} = \left(\frac{D}{E+D}\right)r_d(1 - T_c) + \left(\frac{E}{E+D}\right)r_e.$$ (2.22)

2.3.2 Two-Stage FCFF Model

Once again, if we need to have more flexible forecasts for the firm free cash flow future evolution, we can use two stages with separate growth rates, required rates of return on capital (WACC), and capital reinvestment rates. A straightforward application of all the DCF models in the previous section apply here as well. Suppose that we are forecasting free cash flow to the firm to grow initially at the rate of $g_1 = b_1 \times \text{ROC}_1$ for n periods. Thereafter, the free cash flow to equity is expected to grow at the rate of $g_2 = b_2 \times \text{ROC}_2$ in perpetuity. If the initial free cash flow to equity per share is FCFF_0 and the respective weighted average costs of capital in the two stages are WACC_1 and WACC_2, then the intrinsic equity value per share is given by

$$V_0^F = \frac{\text{FCFF}_0(1+g_1)\left[1 - \left(\frac{1+g_1}{1+\text{WACC}_1}\right)^n\right]}{\text{WACC}_1 - g_1}$$
$$+ \frac{\text{FCFF}_0(1+g_1)^n(1+g_2)}{(\text{WACC}_2 - g_2)(1+\text{WACC}_1)^n}.$$ (2.23)

Note that the first stage is just a growing annuity and, hence, we can have an arbitrarily large g_1 relative to WACC_1. The second stage is a growing perpetuity, so we have to be careful to avoid infinite intrinsic values by making sure that our forecast for g_2 is strictly less than WACC_2.[2]

Once again, a simpler two-stage FCFF model arises if we are willing to assume or forecast a single WACC for both stages and require that the FCFF growth rate undergoes a continuous change between the two stages. Adapting the H model to the case of FCFF leads to

$$V_0^F = \frac{\text{FCFF}_0(1+g_2+(n/2)(g_1-g_2))}{\text{WACC}_1 - g_2}.$$ (2.24)

2.3.3 Three-Stage FCFF Model

Consider next the following set of forecasts for future free cash flow to the firm. Initially, they grow for n_1 periods at the rate of g_1 which attracts a required rate of return on capital of WACC_1. Next, the growth rate in FCFF is forecast to change linearly from g_1 to g_2 over the course of n_2 periods. Finally, this is followed by a perpetual stage of stable growth at the rate of g_2. The transition stage and the stable stage both attract a required rate of return on capital of WACC_2. This gives a terminal value at date n_1 given by

$$V_{n_1}^F = \frac{\text{FCFF}_0(1+g_1)^{n_1}(1+g_2+(n_2/2)(g_1-g_2))}{(\text{WACC}_2-g_2)}. \tag{2.25}$$

Combining this terminal value from H model with the first stage of high growth leads to the following expression for the present intrinsic firm value in this particular three-stage FCFF model:

$$
V_0^F = \frac{\text{FCFF}_0(1+g_1)\left(1-\left(\dfrac{1+g_1}{1+\text{WACC}_1}\right)^{n_1}\right)}{\text{WACC}_1-g_1}
$$
$$
+\frac{\text{FCFF}_0(1+g_1)^{n_1}(1+g_2+(n_2/2)(g_1-g_2))}{(\text{WACC}_2-g_2)(1+\text{WACC}_1)^{n_1}} \tag{2.26}
$$

Occasionally, one might want to have three stages with distinctly different but constant FCFF growth rates for the duration of each stage. Consider a model where initially FCFF are expected to grow at the rate of g_1 for n_1 periods, then at the rate of g_2 for n_2 periods, and finally at the rate of g_3 forever. It is straightforward to show that the present intrinsic firm value in such a three-stage FCFF model is

$$
V_0^F = \frac{\text{FCFF}_0(1+g_1)\left(1-\left(\dfrac{1+g_1}{1+\text{WACC}_1}\right)^{n_1}\right)}{\text{WACC}_1-g_1}
$$
$$
+\frac{V_{n_1}^F}{(1+\text{WACC}_1)^{n_1}}+\frac{V_{n_1+n_2}^F}{(1+\text{WACC}_1)^{n_1}(1+\text{WACC}_2)^{n_2}}, \tag{2.27}
$$

where

$$
V_{n_1}^F = \frac{\text{FCFF}_0(1+g_1)^{n_1}(1+g_2)\left(1-\left(\dfrac{1+g_2}{1+\text{WACC}_2}\right)^{n_2}\right)}{\text{WACC}_2-g_2},
$$

$$
V_{n_1+n_2}^F = \frac{\text{FCFF}_0(1+g_1)^{n_1}(1+g_2)^{n_2}(1+g_3)}{\text{WACC}_3-g_3}
$$

are the present value at $t = 0$ of the third-stage FCFF and the present value at $t = 0$ of the second-stage FCFF, respectively.

Problems

1. Is it always the case that a two-stage model provides a higher value than the one provided by the H model? Assume that the two growth rate forecasts are the same in both models. Try to construct an example and a counterexample.

2. What would it take for FCFE > FCFF in every future period? Is that a sustainable financial strategy?

3. Consider valuing the equity in a firm using a discounted equity-free cash flow model and valuing the equity in the same firm in a slightly roundabout way using a discounted firm cash flow model to value the firm and subtracting the value of the firm's debt from the value of the firm. Under what conditions would the two valuations be identical? Do these conditions make sense?

3

Relative Valuation with Equity and Value Multiples

3.1 Equity Multiples

3.1.1 Price–Dividend Ratio

In theory, the current equity value-to-dividend ratio is obtained by taking the single-stage dividend growth model value of equity per share today, V_0^E, and dividing it by the current dividend per share, D_0:

$$\frac{V_0^E}{D_0} = \frac{(1+g)}{r_e - g}, \tag{3.1}$$

which we can compare to the market price-to-dividend ratio to determine whether the market currently undervalues or overvalues the equity. Note that we can invert this ratio to obtain the current theoretically implied dividend yield as follows:

$$\frac{D_0}{V_0^E} = \frac{r_e - g}{(1+g)}, \tag{3.2}$$

which we can similarly compare to the market-based dividend yield. Similarly, the forward equity value-to-dividend ratio is obtained in the framework of the single-stage dividend growth model equity value and by dividing it by next period's expected dividend per share, D_1:

$$\frac{V_0^E}{D_1} = \frac{1}{r_e - g}, \tag{3.3}$$

giving us the theoretically implied forward dividend yield which we can compare to the analysts' expected consensus forward dividend yield to determine whether the equity is mispriced in the market.

An alternative way of expressing these dividend multiples in terms of yields is also possible. We can also express the future expected dividend yield very intuitively as the difference between the required equity return and the expected dividend growth rate, or the expected capital gain rate, as follows:

$$\frac{D_1}{V_0^E} = r_e - g. \tag{3.4}$$

Note that this equation says nothing more than what we would normally expect, i.e., the required equity return is simply equal to the expected dividend yield plus the expected growth in the dividend yield:

$$r_e = \frac{D_1}{V_0^E} + g. \tag{3.5}$$

3.1.2   Price–Earnings Ratio

If we define the dividend payout ratio (DPY), as the ratio of dividends per share to earnings per share, we can use the single-stage dividend growth model to arrive at the current theoretically implied equity value-to-earnings ratio as a function of the economic fundamentals of the firm:

$$\frac{V_0^E}{E_0} = \frac{DPY_0(1+g)}{r_e - g}. \tag{3.6}$$

Note that this quantity is always increasing in g as long as $g < r_e$ and the growth rate is feasible, i.e., $g = (1 - DPY)ROE$. Similarly, we can express the forward price–earnings ratio as

$$\frac{V_0^E}{E_1} = \frac{DPY_1}{r_e - g}. \tag{3.7}$$

Note that at the sustainable growth rate $g = b \times ROE$, the above expression for the forward PE ratio becomes

$$\frac{V_0^E}{E_1} = \frac{1}{ROE} \frac{ROE - g}{r_e - g} = \frac{V_0^E/BV_0^E}{ROE}. \tag{3.8}$$

It is worth noting that the PE multiples will always increase when the expected earnings reinvestment rate increases even when the return on investment on this incremental investment or ROE is below the required rate of return on equity, r_e. One crude albeit effective way to scale PE multiples for expected future growth rate is to divide them by the expected growth rate leading to the PEG ratio:

$$\text{PEG} = \frac{\text{PE}}{g}. \tag{3.9}$$

In practice, expressing g in decimal format leads to very large values. To deal with this issue, analysts express g in percent which leads to lower numerical values. Note that the lower the PEG ratio is the more undervalued a stock is perceived to be which runs the opposite way of the standard multiples.

An alternative and more general way of expressing these multiples is in the form of earnings yields or the inverse of the price multiples. The current earnings yield of a stock is given by

$$\frac{E_0}{V_0^E} = \frac{r_e - g}{\text{DPY}_0(1+g)}, \tag{3.10}$$

while the forward earnings yield is:

$$\frac{E_1}{V_0^E} = \frac{r_e - g}{\text{DPY}_1}. \tag{3.11}$$

Note that both the current and the forward earnings yields can be negative when the earnings per share are currently negative or are expected to be negative in the next period. However, in practice price–earnings multiples are only computed and reported for stocks that have, or are expected to have, positive earnings per share. Note that this introduces a bias in favor of stocks with positive earnings per share in reported PE multiples. Ideally, we would aggregate the market value of all stocks and divide by the aggregate earnings in order to get a more realistic PE multiple for the entire stock market. This disadvantage does not arise for earnings yields which can be either positive or negative without losing meaning. A negative market price per dollar of earnings, however, makes no economic sense whatsoever.

3.1.3 Price-to-Book Ratio

The value of the current equity value-to-book ratio can be motivated as follows:

$$\frac{V_0^E}{BV_0^E} = \text{ROE} \times \frac{\text{DPY}_0(1+g)}{r_e - g}. \tag{3.12}$$

The forward equity value-to-book ratio results in a more intuitive formula:

$$\frac{V_1^E}{BV_0^E} = \text{ROE} \times \frac{\text{DPY}_1}{r_e - g}, \qquad (3.13)$$

$$= \frac{\text{ROE} - g}{r_e - g}, \qquad (3.14)$$

where the last step takes into account that $g = (1 - \text{DPY}) \times \text{ROE}$. Note that the forward price-to-book ratio is increasing in the expected growth rate g, if and only if $\text{ROE} > r_e$. Alternatively, we can express the last condition as a requirement for the company to earn positive economic profits, i.e., rates of economic profits that exceed the opportunity cost of the next best alternative, the shareholders' required rate of return on equity. Note also the pernicious of pursuing growth for its own sake when the company is failing to earn its required rate of return on equity, $\text{ROE} < r_e$, in which case increasing g will lead to a lower value of the forward price-to-book multiple.

3.1.4 Price–Sales Ratio

The ratio of stock price per share to revenue or sales per share gives us the price-to-revenue ratio or, as it is usually referred to by analysts, the price-to-sales or PS ratio, in short. In theory, there should be a value of equity per share which we can scale by the actual sales per share as follows:

$$\frac{V_0^E}{\text{Sales}_0} = \text{NPM} \times \frac{\text{DPY}_0(1 + g)}{r_e - g}, \qquad (3.15)$$

which we can once again compare to the market PS ratio to determine whether the equity is overvalued or undervalued. Note that the theoretically implied equity value-to-sales multiple is directly proportional to the net profit margin (NPM). It is also proportional to the dividend payout ratio, increasing in the feasible growth rate forecast and decreasing in the require rate of return on equity.

3.2 Value Multiples

Starting with the basic free cash flow to firm valuation, we have that the value of the firm in a single-stage perpetual FCFF growth model is given by

$$V_0^F = \frac{\text{FCFF}_1}{\text{WACC} - g}. \qquad (3.16)$$

3.2.1 Value-to-Income Ratio

Using a simplified version of FCFF linking it to the after-tax operating profit and the capital reinvestment rate, we have

$$\text{FCFF}_1 = (1 - T_c)\text{EBIT}_1 \times (1 - b). \qquad (3.17)$$

Dividing both sides of (3.16) by EBIT$(1 - T_c)$, we get the value–EBIT ratio as follows:

$$\frac{V_0^F}{\text{EBIT}_1} = \frac{(1 - T_c)(1 - b)}{(\text{WACC} - g)}. \qquad (3.18)$$

Occasionally, it is useful to calculate this ratio on an after-tax EBIT basis, which effectively get rid of the T_c in the numerator of the right-hand side.[1] Dividing both sides by $(1 - T_c)$ leads to

$$\frac{V_0^F}{\text{EBIT}_1(1 - T_c)} = \frac{(1 - b)}{(\text{WACC} - g)}.$$

In both case we need to compare these theoretically implied value to their market-based counterparts, the $\text{EV}_0/\text{EBIT}_1$ and the $\text{EV}_0/\text{EBIT}_0(1 - T_c)$, respectively, in order to determine whether the firm is trading at a premium or discount to what can be reasonable to expect based on its economic fundamentals.

3.2.2 Value-to-Book Ratio

The next important value multiple to consider is the firm-level generalization of the price-to-book equity multiple. Starting again with the firm value driven by a single-stage FCFF model:

$$V_0^F = \frac{\text{EBIT}_1(1 - T_c)(1 - b)}{\text{WACC} - g}, \qquad (3.19)$$

and taking into account the link between the feasible growth rate of firm free cash flows, return on capital, and the capital reinvestment rate

$$\text{ROC} = \frac{\text{EBIT}_1(1 - T_c)}{\text{BV}_0}$$

$$b = \frac{g}{\text{ROC}}$$

the theoretically implied firm value-to-book-value multiple can be expressed as

$$\frac{V_0^F}{\text{BV}_0^F} = \frac{\text{ROC} - g}{\text{WACC} - g},$$

which we need to compare to its market counterpart, the EV/BV ratio.

3.2.3   Value-to-Sales Ratio

The final value multiple to consider is the firm-level generalization of the price-to-sales multiple. Note that in contrast to the PS multiple the value-to-sales ratio is uniform and consistent in the sense that both the denominator and the numerator refer to firm-level variables which is not the case for the PS ratio.

In order to derive the value-to-revenue ratio, we start once again with firm value driven by a single-stage FCFF model:

$$V_0^F = \frac{\text{EBIT}_1(1 - T_c)(1 - b)}{\text{WACC} - g}, \tag{3.20}$$

and divide both sides by total sales to obtain

$$\frac{V_0^F}{\text{Sales}_0} = \frac{\dfrac{\text{EBIT}_1(1 - T_c)}{\text{Sales}_0}(1 - b)}{\text{WACC} - g} \tag{3.21}$$

$$= \frac{\text{After-tax operating margin}(1 - b)}{\text{WACC} - g}.$$

Note that the theoretically implied firm value-to-sales ratio is directly proportional to the firm's after-tax operating margin. It is also increasing in the expected FCFF growth rate g. It is decreasing in the capital reinvestment rate and the weighted-average cost of capital. Furthermore, the VS multiple will, typically, exceed the PS ratio provided the firm's net debt is positive. However, for firms whose cash balance exceeds their long-term obligations the VS ratio will be smaller than the PS ratio. Once again, to determine whether the firm's assets are overvalued or undervalued in the marketplace we need to compare the theoretically implied multiple with the market-based EV/sales multiple.

Problems

1. Verify that, all else being equal, the PE ratio increases as the reinvestment rate increases.

2. Verify that, all else being equal, the PB ratio increases as the reinvestment rate increases, provided that $ROE > r_e$.

3. Verify that, all else being equal, the EV/BV ratio increases as the capital reinvestment rate increases, provided that $ROC > WACC$.

4. Consider a company with an ROC of 20%, debt–equity ratio of 1:3, after-tax cost of debt of 6%, cost of equity of 18%, a reinvestment rate of 50%, and an after-tax operating margin of 10%. The marginal corporate income tax rate is 50%. Based on a single-stage FCFF valuation model of this firm, determine what the following value multiples for this company will be equal to

  (a) EV/Book value of capital
  (b) EV/Sales
  (c) EV/EBIT$(1-t)$
  (d) EV/EBIT

4

Financial Options

4.1 Equity Calls and Puts

A call option on a stock entitles the owner to buy the stock at a prespecified price at or before the maturity of the option. This prespecified price at which we can acquire the underlying stock is usually called the exercise price or the strike price. Conversely, a put option on a stock entitles the owner to sell the stock at the strike price at or before maturity of the option. Options that can only be exercised at their maturity dates are referred to as European while options that can be exercised at any time before or at their maturity dates are called American.[1]

A stock option is a legal contract that is essentially a side bet between the buyer and the seller. It has several key quantities that drive the value of the option, namely, the exercise price or the strike price, the time until maturity, and the exercise style. In addition, the prevailing risk-free rate of return as well as the current price and the volatility of the underlying stock price complete the list of variables that determine the value of the option.

After an option has been created, the underlying stock price will typically move around relative to its initial value at inception. The relative position of the current price level of the underlying stock to the strike price determines the moneyness of the option. In particular, call options for which the current stock price, S_t, exceeds the strike price, X, are referred to as being in the money. Similarly, put options for which the current stock price is exceeded by the strike price are also referred to as being in the money. The opposite of an in-the-money option is an option that is out of the money. Finally, if the current price of the underlying stock is exactly equal to the strike price then both the call and put options with that strike price will be at the money.

The monetary payoff to a call option, C_T, and a put option, P_T, that the holder is entitled to receive whenever they are exercised at the maturity date T is as follows:

$$C_T = \max(S_T - X, 0),$$
$$P_T = \max(X - S_T, 0).$$

Figure 4.1 plots the payoff to a European call and put option from the perspective of both the buyer and the seller. A buyer of an option is referred to as being long the option while the option seller is referred to as being short the option. To a buyer, an option delivers a nonnegative payoff that is strictly positive over an extended range of values of the underlying stock price. It is clear that such an asset will command a positive price at inception. Conversely, an option seller is faced with

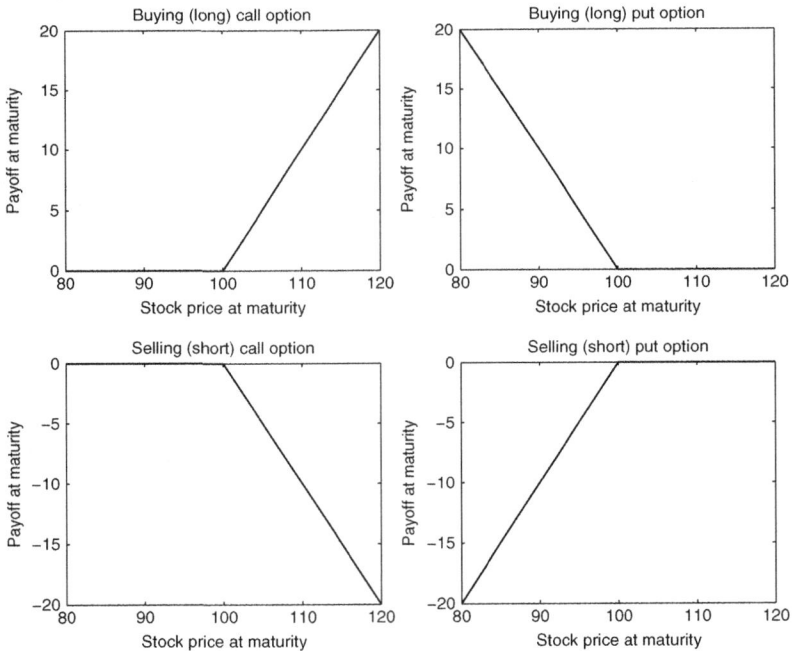

Figure 4.1   Payoff diagrams of call/put options long/short positions.

a nonpositive payoff at the maturity of the option and, thus, the seller will have to be compensated at the inception of the option. Hence, it is clear that options command a positive value at inception. One peculiar difference between call and put options from the point of view of a seller is that a short call option can have, in theory, an unbounded liability to the seller while a short put option has a limited downside as the underlying stock price can be only as far down as zero (assuming the stock is a limited liability asset). Note also that a long option position is a right but not an obligation, i.e., exercising a call that is out of the money is tantamount to throwing away money and is strictly dominated by letting the option to expire worthless. A seller on the other hand may have a contingent liability when the option is in the money at maturity and is forced to deliver or purchase the underlying stock at the prespecified strike price precisely at the point in time when that would lead to a negative payoff to the option seller. The compensation for this to the option seller is the option price received at the inception of the option.

The below table summarizes the rights and contingent obligations to the two counterparties of an option contract:

	Buyer	*Seller*
Call option	Right to buy asset	Obligation to sell asset
Put option	Right to sell asset	Obligation to buy asset

The maturity payoffs of the options depicted above are referred to as the intrinsic value of the options.[2] By now it should be clear that inception options have a positive value and, hence, command a positive price in the option market. The difference between the option market price and the option's intrinsic value is known as the time value of options.[3] A more intuitive way to think about the time value of options is that it represents the extra value received because of the risk that the underlying stock price will move by the time we exercise the option at or before maturity of the option.

Table 4.1 presents some data on listed call options[4] on shares of Microsoft as of December 13, 2005 when the prevailing price per share of Microsoft was $27.45. It is left as an exercise for the reader to determine which options are in the money and what their payoffs would be upon exercise. It is clear that the higher the exercise price is the lower the value of the call option is going to be. Having a

Table 4.1 Call options on Microsoft (Dec. 13, 2005, expire on Friday, Dec. 16, 2005, maturity = 3 days)

Symbol	Strike Price	Last	Volume	Open Interest
MQFLA.X	5.00	22.90	43	43
MQFLU.X	7.50	20.40	43	400
MQFLB.X	10.00	17.60	936	417
MQFLV.X	12.50	15.50	400	400
MQFLC.X	15.00	13.00	99	99
MQFLW.X	17.50	10.30	65	65
MQFLD.X	20.00	7.50	6	261
MSQLX.X	22.50	5.30	1	1,200
MSQLJ.X	25.00	2.45	752	28,264
MSQLY.X	27.50	0.15	6,471	73,943
MSQLK.X	30.00	0.05	70	33,763
MSQLZ.X	32.50	0.05	1	22

Source: http://finance.yahoo.com/q/op?s=MSFT

Table 4.2 Put options on Microsoft (Dec. 13, 2005, expire on Friday, Dec. 16, 2005, maturity = 3 days)

Symbol	Strike Price	Last	Volume	Open Interest
MQFXA.X	5.00	0.00	0	0
MQFXU.X	7.50	0.00	0	0
MQFXB.X	10.00	0.00	0	0
MQFXV.X	12.50	0.00	0	0
MQFXC.X	15.00	0.00	0	0
MQFXW.X	17.50	0.00	0	0
MQFXD.X	20.00	0.00	0	0
MSQXX.X	22.50	0.05	20	13,041
MSQXJ.X	25.00	0.05	1	10,327
MSQXY.X	27.50	0.20	1849	22,589
MSQXK.X	30.00	2.60	326	3,080
MSQXZ.X	32.50	4.70	20	0

Source: http://finance.yahoo.com/q/op?s=MSFT

Note: MSFT's stock price before the NYSE open on Dec. 13, 2005 was $27.45.

right to buy the same asset at a higher prespecified price will be worthless. Conversely, having the right to purchase the underlying security cheaper will be worth more.

Table 4.2 presents the last prices of put options on Microsoft shares at various strike prices. As can be readily seen put options with higher strike prices tend to be worth more compared to put options with lower strike prices.

It is also instructive to take a look at the available put options on shares of Microsoft and their prices prevailing on December 13, 2005.

4.2   Examples of Option Strategies

4.2.1   A Protective Put Strategy

Consider the goal of protecting the value of a risky asset, that is, in–out possession. In particular, suppose we are long a stock and we are concerned with a fall in value below a certain number, say $55 per share. One way to achieve such a minimum value is to essentially purchase insurance, in the form of a put option, with a strike price of $55. Therefore, the protective put option strategy will consist of buying one share of stock and one put option on that stock with strike price of $55. The below table depicts the value of the combined position at the maturity of the put option:

	Stock Price < $55	Stock Price ≥ $55
Value of stock	Stock price	Stock price
Value of put option	$55– Stock price	0
Total value	$55	Stock price

Note that we have effectively managed to remove the downside risk at, potentially, a considerable cost depending on the current value of the put option. The payoff of the protective put strategy at the maturity of the put option is depicted in Figure 4.2.

4.2.2   A Straddle Example

The protective put option strategy we have just considered gives rise to an even better and more expensive strategy. We know from previous sections that the payoff of a call option is increasing the underlying stock price at the maturity of the call option. Consider taking the protective put option example we have just considered and adding a call option on the same stock and with the same maturity date and a strike price of $55. This type of strategy will have a strictly positive payoff at the maturity of both options as long as the underlying stock

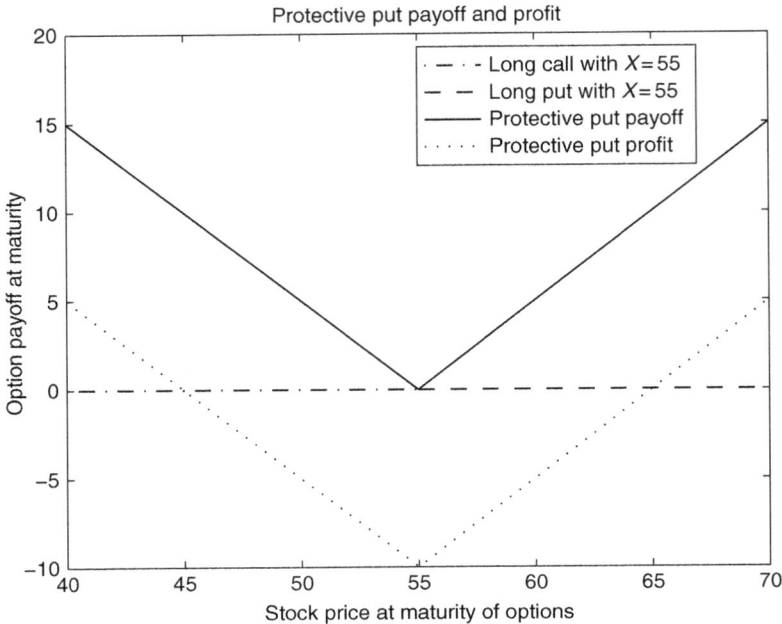

Figure 4.2   Payoffs of protective put.

price finishes away from $55 on the maturity date. This type of an option strategy is referred to as a straddle. It is clearly a profitable strategy as long as the underlying stock price is volatile. It represents an almost certain way of profiting from volatility.

Building on the protective put example from the previous subsection, consider buying one call option with a strike price of $55 and one put option with a strike price of $55 as well as one share of stock. Figure 4.3 depicts the payoffs of the two options as well as the profit of the straddle strategy at the maturity of the options.

Note that the payoff of the straddle strategy is always nonnegative but the profit can turn negative if the underlying stock price does not move sufficiently away from the common strike price of the call and the put. In particular, the stock price has to move further away from the strike by an amount equal to the combined purchase cost of the call and the put option in order for the profit to turn positive.

This strategy will have a higher likelihood of turning in a positive profit during particularly volatile times or especially for volatile

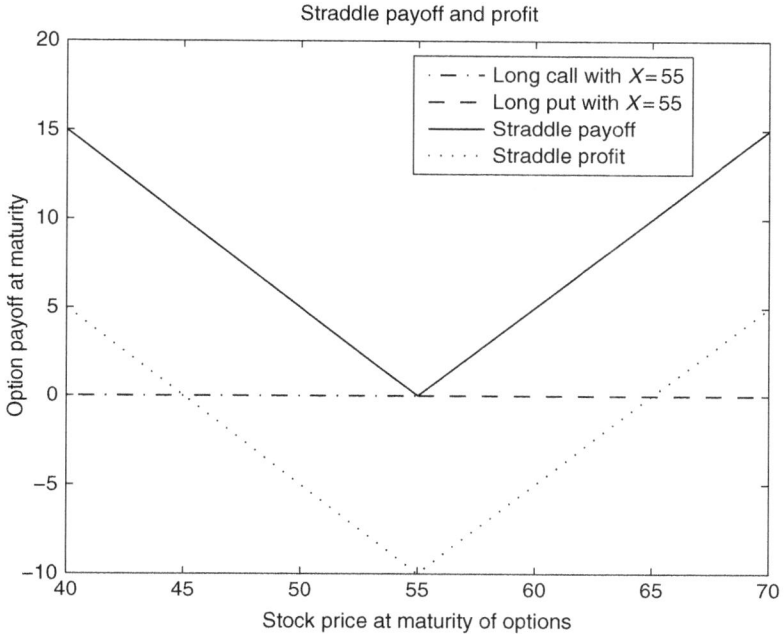

Figure 4.3   Payoffs of straddle option strategy.

stocks. Conversely, in a sideways market when volatility is low one may consider taking the opposite side and selling the straddle. Note, however, that this is especially risky in case the underlying stock price has a sudden large move and either of the two options will trigger a contingent obligation to deliver the underlying stock at a loss to the straddle seller.

4.2.3   A Butterfly Example

Consider now a combination of three options with three different strikes. For the purposes of this example, we will take three options with equally spaced strike prices. Consider call options first. If we purchase the call with the smallest strike and the one with the largest strike while selling two calls with the intermediate strike price, we can deliver a nonnegative payoff at maturity which is strictly positive in the range of values of the underlying strike price in between the two outermost strikes. In order to avoid an arbitrage opportunity, such an option combination has to attract a positive cost of out pocket at the

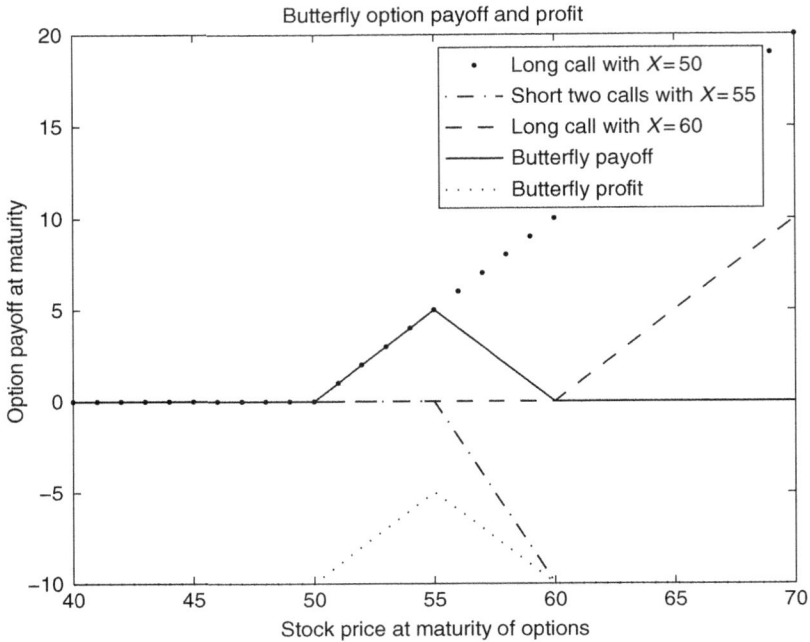

Figure 4.4 Payoffs of butterfly option strategy (calls).

time we put the butterfly strategy in place. The same ideas work if we replace the call options with put options.

Figure 4.4 plots the payoff and profit of a butterfly strategy using call options with strike prices of 50, 55, and 60. In order to obtain the butterfly payoff, we need to purchase 50 and 60 calls and sell 2 of the 55 calls. This produces a nonnegative payoff at the maturity of the call options which is strictly positive when the underlying stock price finishes up anywhere between 50 and 60 at the maturity of the options.

Figure 4.5 depicts the payoff and profit of the butterfly strategy implemented with put options with strike prices of 50, 55, and 60. The logic of the butterfly strategy with puts is the same as the butterfly strategy with calls. Note that the net payoff is identical to the one that obtains with call options.

The intuition behind the absence of arbitrage condition on the three call options and the three put options that are part of the butterfly

Butterfly option payoff and profit

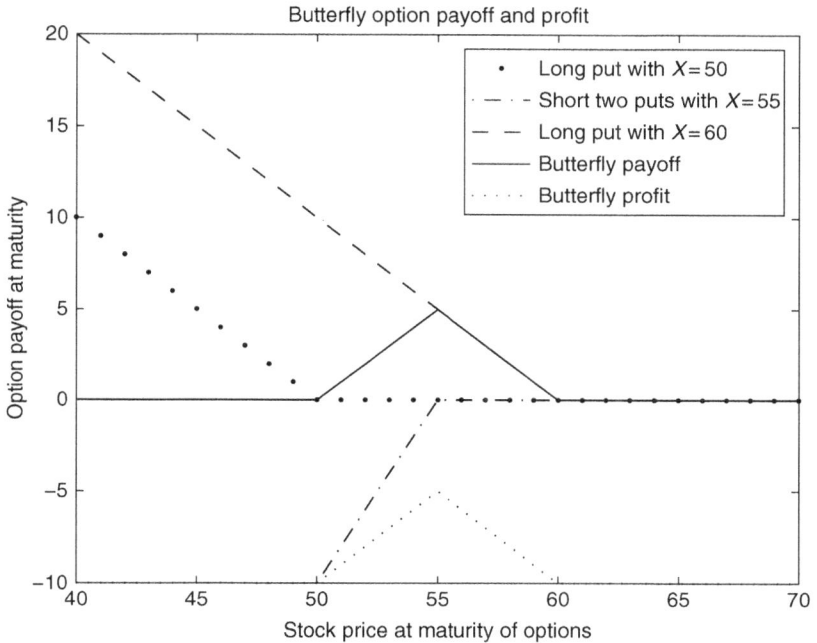

Figure 4.5 Payoffs of butterfly option strategy (puts).

strategy is a simple statement about the convexity of the option value as the underlying stock price changes at the maturity of the options. Convexity requires that the average price of the 50 and 60 call (put) must exceed the actual price of the 55 call (put). If the opposite holds, then the option value is no longer convex but is instead concave which makes no sense given the convex piecewise linear payoffs of call and put options.

4.3 Option Valuation

There are two primary methods for option valuation. One involves continuous time mathematics and stochastic processes while the other one involves binomial trees. The latter is more intuitive and allows us to value some options that are impossible to value in the continuous time framework, so we will focus primarily on the binomial option pricing method in this section. The limit of the binomial option pricing

method as the length of the time interval decreases to zero does lead
to the continuous time limit, so there is no loss of generality.

4.3.1 Bounds on Option Values

Before we proceed to formally derive option values, it is worthwhile
to consider some rough bounds on the values of options. Let us first
consider the case of call options. It is clear from the terminal payoff
that when the stock price is worthless at the maturity of the option,
the option will be worth nothing as well. At the opposite extreme,
when the stock price becomes extremely expensive the option is worth
approximately the stock price minus the present value of the strike
price. The option value prior to maturity always exceeds the terminal
payoff though sometimes the time value can be quite small when the
option is out of the money. Furthermore, it makes sense that the longer
we have this valuable right for, the more valuable the right will be.
Similarly, if the underlying stock price is very volatile it gives us a

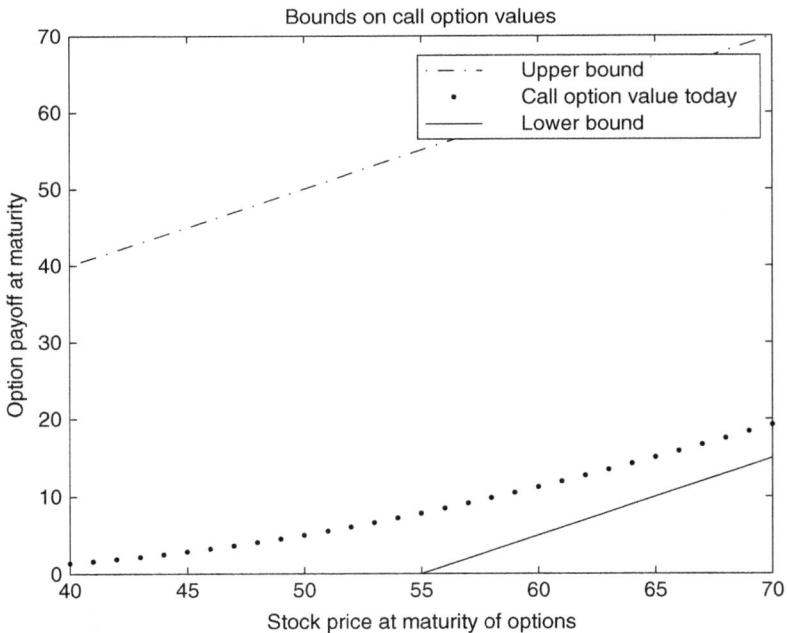

Figure 4.6 Upper and lower limits on option values.

bigger chance of maturing deep in the money and, hence, delivering a large terminal payoff. Therefore, it stands to reason that options on more volatile stocks will be worth more.

Figure 4.6 illustrates some of these limiting values by plotting the value of a call option at inception versus its intrinsic value at maturity as a function of the terminal stock price.

Furthermore, it should be clear from the call option payoff that if the strike price increases then the call option is worth less. This makes perfect sense if we recall that this situation involves having a right to acquire the underlying stock at a higher prespecified price so such a right will be worth less to use today than an otherwise comparable right allowing us to acquire the asset for less. What is less obvious is that when interest rates increase this renders call options more valuable.

The sensitivity of put option values to time to maturity and stock price volatility is identical to the same sensitivities for call options. All the other sensitivities of put option values are the opposite of the sensitivities of call option values. We will soon be able to formally prove all of these claims.

Before we continue to the option valuation stage, it is worthwhile to consider the wide array of financial assets with various degrees of explicit or implicit optionality built into them. Plain vanilla call and put options are side bets and do not involve changing the number of underlying shares of stock. However, warrants work just like calls and put but involve instead a change in the number of shares issued and outstanding. Furthermore, corporate bonds can be callable or puttable (or both) as well as convertible into shares of common stock in the same company. A mortgage that can be prepaid essentially contains a put option on behalf of the mortgagee. Furthermore, a wide variety of more general decisions involve options that are termed real options. These include, but are not limited to, the option to expand, the option to abandon, the option to vary capacity, etc. We shall encounter all of these options later on and try to figure out a way to determine the value of all of them.

4.4 Option Pricing

The basic idea underpinning binomial option pricing is quite simple and intuitive. Essentially, we are going to price the derivative security as a redundant security by constructing a replicating portfolio that is a perfect hedge for the value of the derivative. Then we are going to argue that the value of the derivative today has to be equal to the value of the replicating portfolio today. Any other derivative value will lead to an arbitrage opportunity which will allow an arbitrageur to create a risk-free profit opportunity. The replicating portfolio will consist of buying and selling the underlying security and risk-free borrowing or lending as the case might be.

Let us start with the simplest two-date two-state version of the binomial option pricing model. Consider a risky stock that is currently trading at $100 at $t = 0$ and will have a market value of either $200 in the up state or $50 in the down state at $t = 1$. Similarly, we observe a one-period zero-coupon risk-free bond with a face value of $100 payable at $t = 1$ and currently trading at $90 at $t = 0$. We are trying to construct a portfolio that has to replicate the payoffs of a call option on the stock with a strike price of $100. The values and payoffs of all three securities are as follows:

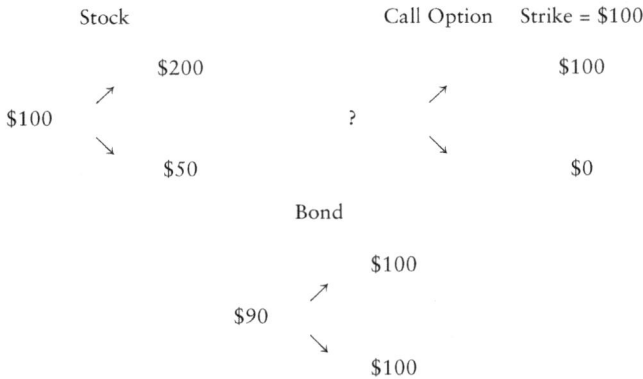

In order to do this, we need some notation. Let N_S be the number of shares of stock in the replicating portfolio and N_B be number of bonds that we will use in replicating the option's payoffs. A perfect replicating portfolio is one that has the exact same values in both states at $t = 1$ as the call option we are trying to price. This leads us to the following system of linear equations we need to solve:

$$200 \times N_S + 100 \times N_B = 100,$$

$$50 \times N_S + 100 \times N_B = 0.$$

The solution is given by $N_S = \frac{2}{3}$ and $N_B = -\frac{1}{3}$. In other words, in order to replicate three options, we need to buy two shares of stock and sell one bond. Note that the replicating portfolio involves leverage and consists of buying the risky underlying stock partially funding the purchase with risk-free borrowing. This is the general result for all plain vanilla call options.

The value of the call option today at $t = 0$ must equal the value of the replicating portfolio at $t = 0$ or

$$\text{Call option value}_0 = 100 \times \left(\frac{2}{3}\right) + 90 \times \left(-\frac{1}{3}\right) = 36.67.$$

The value of the call option cannot be higher. Suppose for the sake of argument that the call option was trading at $40. In this case, we can sell the call option and invest $36.67 in the replicating portfolio at $t = 0$. We liquidate the replicating portfolio at $t = 1$ and make the required payoffs. This means we had a risk-free profit at $t = 0$ equal to $3.33. We can argue in a similar fashion that the value of the call option cannot be lower than $36.67. Suppose that the market value of the call was $35. Then we can buy the call option and sell the replicating portfolio. At $t = 1$, we collect the option payoffs and cover perfectly any liabilities arising from selling the replicating portfolio. Hence, we have made a risk-free arbitrage profit of $1.67. The only value for the call option at which this arbitrage profit opportunity disappears is the value of the replicating portfolio.

Consider next how we would value a put option with a strike price of $100 written on the same stock as the call option we priced previously. The payoffs of all three securities are stated as follows:

Let us construct a system of two equations again using both the stock and the risk-free bond that replicates the value of the put option exactly in both states of the world at $t = 1$:

$$200 \times N_S + 100 \times N_B = 0,$$
$$50 \times N_S + 100 \times N_B = 50.$$

The solution in this case is given by $N_S = -(1/3)$ and $N_B = +(2/3)$. This means that in order to replicate 3 put options we need to sell short 1 share of stock and buy 2 bonds. Replicating the payoff of the put option involves selling short the underlying security and investing the proceeds of the short sale at the risk-free rate. Note that the replicating portfolio for put options is quite different from the one for call options. The value of the put option today must be equal to the value of the replicating portfolio:

$$\text{Put option value}_0 = 100 \times \left(-\frac{1}{3}\right) + 90 \times \left(+\frac{2}{3}\right) = 26.67.$$

Now we are in a position to evaluate the cost of the option strategies mentioned in the previous section. For example, investing in a protective put option strategy will cost us \$26.67. Investing in a straddle volatility bet (buying 1 call and 1 put) will cost us \$36.67 + \$26.67 = \$63.34.

Armed with the option replicating portfolio, it is easy to see how useful it can be for risk-management and hedging purposes. If an investor owns an option and needs to unload the entire risk of the option, then all that she needs to do is to sell the underlying replicating portfolio. The remaining position will be risk-free and will yield risk-free rates of return.

In theory, we can also use the expected NPV rule to figure out the price of an option. However, we would need to know the right risk-adjusted discount rate. This gets even more complicated as the discount rate changes over the life of the option as the replicating portfolio becomes dynamic. The discount rate also changes as the underlying asset value changes.

In order to gain more intuition into the pricing of options, we introduce a bit more notation. Suppose that the value of the market value at $t = 0$ of the risky underlying security is equal to S_0, the risk-free zero-coupon bond's value is B_0, and the option value is O_0. The risk-free interest rate per period is given by R. Over the next period, the stock price can go up by U percent in the "up" state of the world or it can go down by D percent in the "down" state of the world. The values and payoffs of all three securities are illustrated below:

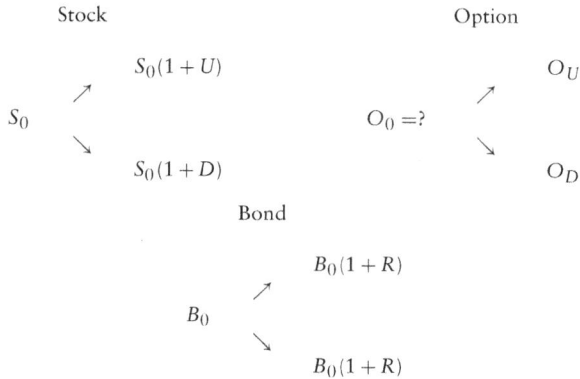

Stock

$$S_0(1+U)$$

$$S_0 \nearrow$$
$$\searrow$$

$$S_0(1+D)$$

Option

$$O_U$$

$$O_0 =? \nearrow$$
$$\searrow$$

$$O_D$$

Bond

$$B_0(1+R)$$

$$B_0 \nearrow$$
$$\searrow$$

$$B_0(1+R)$$

At this level of generality, a very important point needs to be made that we are not entirely free in our choice of values, particularly, the values of U, D, and R. We need to make sure that there is no arbitrage built into the model of the stock price and the bond price before we can even price the option. To see this, suppose that $U > D > R$. In this case, the returns of the risky security always exceed the risk-free rate in both states of the world. Hence, an arbitrage trade would involve borrowing at the risk-free rate, i.e., selling short the zero-coupon risk-free bond, and investing the proceeds in the risky stock. This trade is guaranteed to make money and is self-financing in that we do not risk any of our own money. Hence, this particular inequality for the parameter value is not arbitrage-free. Next, suppose that $R > U > D$. In this case, the return of the risk-free bond dominates the returns of the risky security in both states of the world. An arbitrage strategy here would involve selling short the risky underlying security and investing the proceeds in the risk-free bond. We are guaranteed to make a profit in both states of the world and, once again, we are not risking anything. Therefore, this inequality is also untenable. The only viable arbitrage-free condition for the parameters of the binomial option pricing model is the following:

$U > R > D.$

Proceeding under the assumption that all our binomial option pricing models will have to fulfill the above condition, we continue with the setup of a replicating strategy in this more general case. Once again, we require that the replicating portfolio matches exactly the payoffs of the option in the up state, O_U, as well as the down state, O_D. This leads to the following system of linear equations for N_S and N_B:

$$S_0(1+U) \times N_S + B_0(1+R) \times N_B = O_U, \tag{4.1}$$

$$S_0(1+D) \times N_S + B_0(1+R) \times N_B = O_D. \tag{4.2}$$

The solution is now given by

$$N_S = \frac{O_U - O_D}{S_0(U-D)}, \tag{4.3}$$

$$N_B = \frac{O_D(1+U) - O_U(1+D)}{B_0(1+R)(U-D)}. \tag{4.4}$$

Using these values for N_S and N_B to evaluate the current value of the replicating portfolio at $t = 0$, after certain simplifications, leads to the following result:

$$O_0 = \left(\frac{1}{1+R}\right)\left[\left(\frac{R-D}{U-D}\right) \times O_U + \left(\frac{U-R}{U-D}\right) \times O_D\right], \tag{4.5}$$

which, after some additional notation, becomes more familiar:

$$O_0 = \left(\frac{1}{1+R}\right)(p^* \times O_U + (1-p^*) \times O_D), \tag{4.6}$$

where p^* is the risk-neutral probability:

$$p^* = \frac{R-D}{U-D}. \tag{4.7}$$

As long as $U > R > D$ (out initial requirement on the model), then we have that

$$0 < p^* < 1,$$

and the risk-neutral probability is a proper probability.

Another concept that is sometimes useful in option pricing and, more generally, in asset pricing, is the state price today at $t = 0$ of $1 to be received at some state in the future. In the context of our two-state single-period model, we can define $PV\$1_U$ as the price today at $t = 0$ of $1 receivable in the up state only at $t = 1$. Similarly, define $PV\$1_D$ as the price today at $t = 0$ of $1 receivable in the down state only at $t = 1$. We can then reexpress the value of any option today as follows:

$$O_0 = PV\$1_U \times O_U + PV\$1_D \times O_D, \tag{4.8}$$

where

$$PV\$1_U = \left(\frac{1}{1+R}\right) p^{*}, \tag{4.9}$$

$$PV\$1_D = \left(\frac{1}{1+R}\right)(1-p^{*}). \tag{4.10}$$

Next, we turn out attention to multiperiod binomial option pricing. For ease of illustration, we shall focus on a three-date, three-state, two-period model and mention how the idea generalizes to any number of periods. Consider first a numerical example where the risky security can increase by 50% ($U = 0.5$) or decrease by 25% ($D = -0.25$) and the risk-free rate per period is 12.5% ($R = 0.125$). The initial stock price is $100, the bond price at $t = 0$ is $80, and we have to price a European put option on the stock with a strike price of $120 ($X = 120$) and two periods to maturity. The values and payoffs of all three securities are illustrated below:

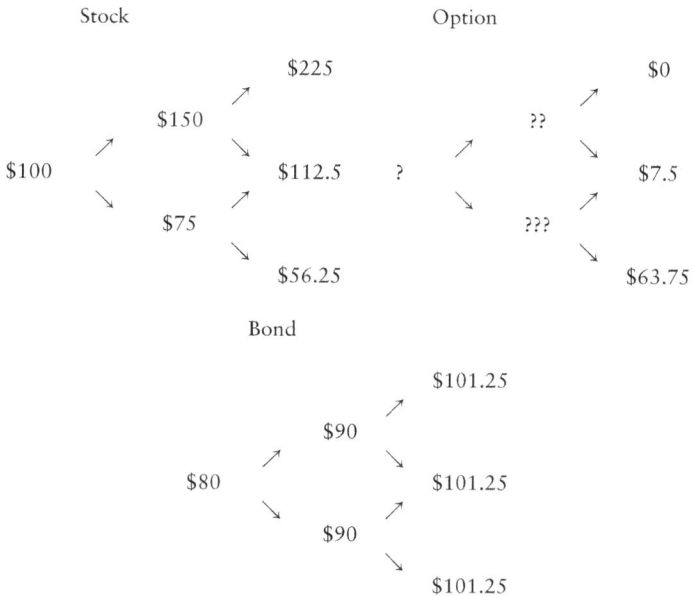

It is easy to verify that for this model the risk-neutral probability is equal to 50% in either state and that both state prices are equal to 4/9:

$$p^* = 0.5\, PV\$1_U = \tfrac{4}{9},$$
$$1 - p^* = 0.5\, PV\$1_D = \tfrac{4}{9}.$$

The first step in this multiperiod binomial option valuation is to apply the two-period result in reducing the $t = 2$ put option payoffs to values at $t = 1$ as follows:

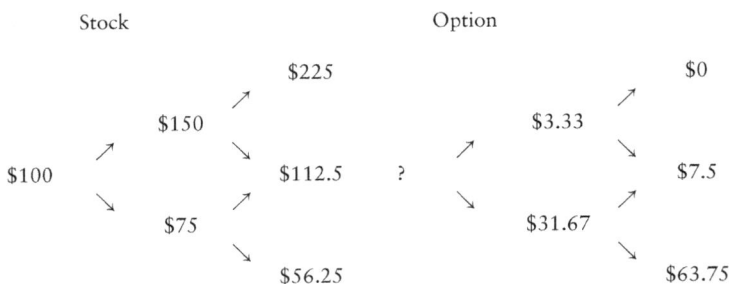

Stock   Option

		$225			$0
	$150			$3.33	
$100		$112.5	?		$7.5
	$75			$31.67	
		$56.25			$63.75

The final step involves taking the $t = 1$ put option values and applying the two-state valuation formula to arrive at the $t = 0$ value for the European put option:

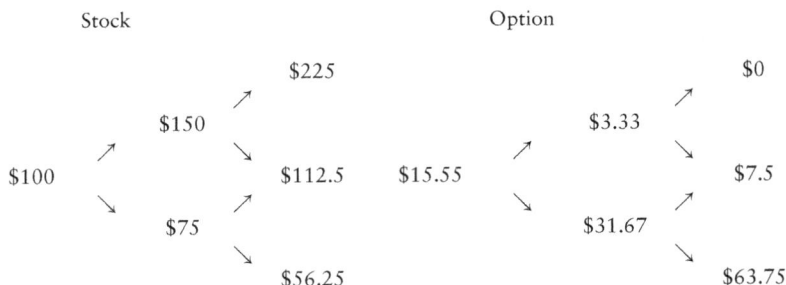

Stock   Option

		$225			$0
	$150			$3.33	
$100		$112.5	$15.55		$7.5
	$75			$31.67	
		$56.25			$63.75

One possibility of obtaining better and better approximations is to continue subdividing into more and more subperiods holding the time to maturity fixed. In the limit, when we have continuous trading there is a closed-form formula for the valuation of European calls, C_t and puts, P_t due to Black and Scholes (1973):

$$C_t = S_t N(d_1) - X e^{-r(T-t)} N(d_2),$$
$$P_t = X e^{-r(T-t)} N(-d_2) - S_t N(-d_1),$$

where S_t is the current underlying stock price, X is the exercise/strike price, r is the risk-free rate, T is the point in time of maturity, $T-t$ is referred to as time to maturity, and $N(\cdot)$ is the cumulative standard normal distribution. The definitions for the remaining terms are as follows:

$$d_1 = \frac{\ln\left(\frac{S_t}{X}\right) + \left(r + \frac{1}{2}\sigma^2\right)(T-t)}{\sigma\sqrt{(T-t)}},$$
$$d_2 = d_1 - \sigma\sqrt{(T-t)},$$
$$N(-d_1) = 1 - N(d_1),$$
$$N(-d_2) = 1 - N(d_2),$$

where σ is the standard deviation of the continuously compounded stock return. Note that the expected stock return never appears in any of these formulas. The reason for this is that the replicating portfolio argument builds a perfect hedge leaving no residual risk.

The power of the binomial option pricing model is illustrated when considering the pricing of American-type exercise options for which no formula can be obtained in continuous time. Nevertheless, such options are straightforward to price in the binomial framework. To continue with our previous put option example, suppose that we can now exercise the put early if it is beneficial to us. The payoffs and values of the American put are illustrated below:

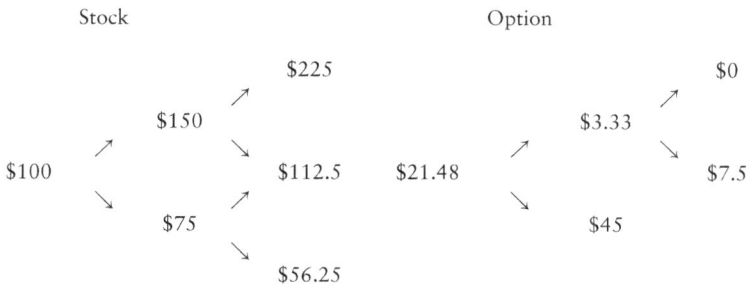

Stock			Option		
		$225			$0
	$150			$3.33	
$100		$112.5	$21.48		$7.5
	$75				$45
		$56.25			

Note that the early exercise in the down state at $t = 1$ is the end of life for the American put and there are no further payoffs. In the up state in the middle date, however, it is worthwhile to keep the American put alive. The difference between the values of the otherwise identical American and European put is sometimes referred to as the early exercise premium, which in this case is equal to $21.48 − $15.55 = $5.93. The longer the time to maturity of the American put, the greater the early exercise premium.

The primary reason we are able to construct a perfect replicating portfolio and a beautiful formula like the Black and Scholes (1973) result is that we are operating in a complete market. What this means is that we have two securities and two states of the world. The returns of the two securities are linearly independent. This property of the market will let us match any possible payoff that is a function of the terminal stock price or, in fact, the entire path of the evolution of the stock price. There is a very important theorem in finance called the fundamental theorem of asset pricing which states that the following four claims are equivalent: (1) asset markets are arbitrage-free, (2) asset markets are complete (in the sense mentioned previously), (3) there exist unique risk-neutral probabilities (p_s^*), and (4) there exist positive state prices $(PV\$1_s)$. The proof of this theorem is beyond the scope of this text but we can make ample use of it in building binomial trees. All we need to do to insure that there is no arbitrage built into the binomial model from the get go is that the risk-neutral probabilities are proper probabilities, i.e., $0 < p^* < 1$, or that the state prices are strictly positive and sum up to at most 1.

Problems

1. Consider the Microsoft call and put options in Tables 4.1 and 4.2, respectively. Assume that they are European and that you can freely trade at the last price listed. Try to find an arbitrage with triplets of consecutive strike prices based on the notion that a butterfly option strategy has to have a strictly positive price at inception.

2. In the context of the single-period binomial option pricing valuation approach, a stock is currently trading at 6 and will be worth either 9 or 4 next year. A quadratic derivative with 1 year to maturity has a terminal payoff of $O_1 = (S_1)^2$ next year. Find the replicating portfolio of this quadratic derivative.

3. Shares in stock A are currently trading at 50 and call option written on A with a strike price of 21 is currently trading at 36. Stock A is expected to be worth either 90 or 40 next year. Find the 1-year risk-free interest rate.

4. Consider the following incomplete market example. A stock currently worth 100 is going to be worth either 120 or 80 in the next period. Based on a superreplicating and a subreplicating portfolio, find the lowest and the highest feasible values of the risk-free rate.

5

Real Options

5.1 Equity and Bond Pricing as Options on Assets

Suppose that the assets of the firms follow a two-state binomial model:

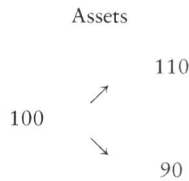

Assets

$$
100 \nearrow \begin{array}{c} 110 \\[1em] \searrow \\ 90 \end{array}
$$

The one-period risk-free rate is 5%. It is straightforward to show that $p_u^* = 0.75$ and $p_d^* = 0.25$. The company has a zero-coupon bond with one period to maturity and face value of 100. Given the possible asset values, the payoffs to the corporate bond are

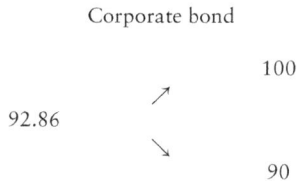

Corporate bond

$$
92.86 \nearrow \begin{array}{c} 100 \\[1em] \searrow \\ 90 \end{array}
$$

The value of the corporate bond today is

$$
\left(\frac{1}{1.05}\right)(0.75 \times 100 + 0.25 \times 90) = 92.86 \tag{5.1}
$$

and has a yield to maturity of 7.69% (a default premium of 2.69%). The company also has equity outstanding, the payoffs for which are given as follows:

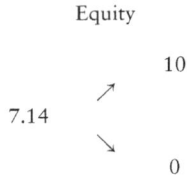

Equity

10

7.14   ↗

↘

0

The value of the equity today is

$$\left(\frac{1}{1.05}\right)(0.75 \times 10 + 0.25 \times 0) = 7.14. \tag{5.2}$$

Note that the sum of the values of equity and the corporate bond $(92.86 + 7.14)$ is exactly equal to the value of assets today (100).

Increasing the risk-free interest rate from 5% to 6% leads to a corporate bond value today that is reduced to 92.45, a yield to maturity of 8.16%, and a default premium of 2.16%. Equity value today increases to 7.55. Alternatively, increasing the asset variance (value up is 120, value down is 80) leads to a reduced corporate bond value today of 88.10 leading to a yield to maturity of 13.51% and a default premium of 8.51%. The new equity value today increases to 11.90.

One could calculate and estimate alternative sensitivities, which can be a little counterintuitive when compared to the DCF valuation paradigm. For example, a small increase in the risk-free interest rate will make the stock worth more today and the corporate bond worth less. Similarly, extending the life of the assets to two periods will increase the value of the stock since it is effectively a call option and decrease the value of the corporate bond. The promised yield to maturity of the corporate bond can go either way though depending on the face value relative to the specific asset values in the future states of the world.

5.2   Pricing Convertible Bonds

Suppose that the assets of the firm are driven by a two-state binomial model and the risk-free rate of interest is equal to zero.

Assets

$$120$$

$$100 \nearrow$$
$$\searrow$$

$$80$$

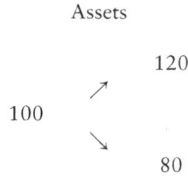

In this case the asset return in the up state is equal to 0.2, or 20%, while the asset return in the down state is equal to -0.2, or -20%. As the risk-free rate is equal to 0, then it is straightforward to show that $p_u^* = 0.5$ and $p_d^* = 0.5$. The company has a zero-coupon convertible bond with one period to maturity and face value of 100. The bond is convertible into 11 shares of common stock at the maturity of the bond at the option of the bondholder. If we assume initially that there is no conversion, then the payoffs of the corporate bond are 100 in the up state and 80 in the down state. The value of the corporate bond today is

$$\left(\frac{1}{1+0}\right)(0.5 \times 100 + 0.5 \times 80) = 90. \tag{5.3}$$

The yield to maturity of the bond is equal to 11.11% resulting in a default premium or a credit spread of 11.11%.

Next, we consider the case where bondholders convert their corporate bonds whenever it is beneficial to them. Note that in the down state the equity is worthless so bondholders will not convert. However, in the up state it is optimal for them to exercise the conversion option even in the face of a dilution of the value of equity. In this case, the payoffs to the convertible corporate bond are 110 in the up state as bondholders convert and 80 in the down state as bondholders do not convert as follows:

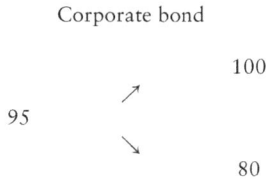

Corporate bond

$$100$$

$$95 \nearrow$$
$$\searrow$$

$$80$$

The value of the convertible corporate bond today is

$$\left(\frac{1}{1+0}\right)(0.5 \times 110 + 0.5 \times 80) = 95, \tag{5.4}$$

resulting in a yield to maturity equal to 5.26% and a default premium or a credit spread of 5.26%.

The company also has equity outstanding, the payoffs for which are given as follows:

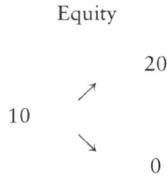

Equity

$$
10 \quad \nearrow \quad \begin{array}{c} 20 \\ \\ \searrow \quad 0 \end{array}
$$

The value of the equity today, assuming no conversion, is

$$
\left(\frac{1}{1+0}\right)(0.5 \times 20 + 0.5 \times 0) = 10. \tag{5.5}
$$

The value of the equity today with optimal conversion by the bondholders is

$$
\left(\frac{1}{1+0}\right)(0.5 \times 10 + 0.5 \times 0) = 5. \tag{5.6}
$$

Note that the sum of the values of equity and the convertible corporate bond (95+5) is exactly equal to the value of assets today (100).

5.3   Option to Wait

Suppose that installing a solar panel today at $t = 0$ on the roof of your house costs 4000. Next year, the expected savings from this investment can be either 300 or 100 with equal probability. For simplicity, we assume that those savings will be realized in perpetuity. The opportunity cost of your capital is 5% and, hence, the DCF value of investing immediately is given by

$$
0.5 \times \frac{300}{0.05} + 0.5 \times \frac{100}{0.05} - 4000 = 0. \tag{5.7}
$$

Hence, we might be indifferent between investing or not investing at time period 0.

Next, consider waiting until next year and deciding whether to invest or not at $t = 1$ depending on the expected cost savings realized at that point in time. The benefit of this is that you will know for sure whether the expected cost savings are equal to 300 or 100. For simplicity, assume that the cost of the solar panel is the same next year (this is not a critical assumption). We realize that it does not pay to invest in the solar panel if the expected cost savings are equal to 100 as the DCF value then is equal to

$$\frac{100}{0.05} - 4000 = -2000 < 0. \tag{5.8}$$

However, it does pay to invest in the up state as the DCF value then is equal to

$$\frac{300}{0.05} - 4000 = 2000. \tag{5.9}$$

The value of this optimal strategy as of time $t = 0$ is equal to

$$0.5 \times \frac{2000}{1.05} = 952.38. \tag{5.10}$$

This is the value today of the optimal real option to wait until you invest. As an exercise, you should consider the more general optimal investment timing problem where the expected savings at time period $t = 2$ are either 400, 200, or 0 with 25%, 50%, and 25% probability, respectively. You should be able to conclude that, from the point of view of $t = 0$, it is optimal to wait only one period before you decide whether to invest. Waiting 2 years is suboptimal as the increased in expected savings are outweighed by having to wait for two periods before investing. Note also that considering the value of the option to wait gives us a considerably different value of this investment project compared to the DCF net present value.

5.4   Option to Abandon

Consider an asset with an uncertain future value. An abandonment option is effectively a put option allowing the holder to sell the underlying asset for a prespecified strike price up until a certain future date. Let us illustrate this with a specific example. Suppose that the future evolution of the asset price follows the following two-period binomial tree. For simplicity, let the physical or objective probability of each branch in the tree be 50%.

Asset

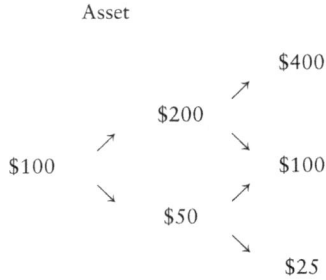

Imagine that the owner of the asset is in a position to sell the asset at any point in time for $100. The owner has a cost of capital of 25%. When would she like to exercise her abandonment option and in what states of the world? A cursory look at the binomial tree reveals that the abandonment option is in the money in the middle period and down state of the world when the asset value is $50 as well as in the last period when the asset value is $25. However, it is not immediately clear which of the two alternatives yields a higher present value. Exercising as soon as it is profitable to do so leads to a higher present value. At the same time, waiting longer before exercising can generate a potentially higher payoff albeit at a later point in time. In order to trade these two opposing forces off, we need to consider the present values of both scenarios.

Suppose first that the asset owner exercises the abandonment option when the asset value is $50. This leads to probability-weighted present value of

$$\frac{1}{2} \times \frac{(100 - 50)}{1.25} = 20. \tag{5.11}$$

The second alternative would be to wait for two periods on the off chance that the asset value drops to $25. The probability-weighted present value of this alternative course of action is

$$\frac{1}{4} \times \frac{100 - 25}{(1.25)^2} = 12. \tag{5.12}$$

Clearly, when the cost of capital is as high as we assumed in this example, the asset owner would be induced to act quickly and exercise the abandonment option as soon as it is in the money. All other things being equal, asset owners will lower opportunity costs of capital will tend to wait longer. Note also how the intuition we have developed about option values carries over to real option values as well. More volatile asset values will result in more valuable abandonment options, etc.

Problems

1. Blacksnake Corp. currently has assets with a market value of 142. Next year, the market value of Blacksnake's assets is going to be equal to 160, 100, or 40 depending on the state of the economy. At the same time, the current value of a stock market index is 1460. Next year, the stock market index will have a value of 1600, 1000, or 800, depending on the state of the economy. The annual risk-free rate of interest is 0%. Blacksnake Corp. has one equity share issued and outstanding as well as one zero-coupon corporate bond outstanding with a face value of 90 which matures next year. Find the value today of Blacksnake's corporate bond and equity share.

2. Distress, Inc. currently has assets with a market value of 100. Next year, the market value of the assets of Distress, Inc. is going to increase by 25% or decrease by 25% depending on the state of the economy. The annual risk-free rate of interest is 0%. Distress, Inc. has one equity share issued and outstanding as well as one zero-coupon corporate bond outstanding with a face value of 100 which matures next year and is callable by the firm next year at a call price of 99.

   (a) Find the value today of the corporate bond of Distress, Inc.
   (b) Suppose the creditors of Distress, Inc. manage to convince management to remove the callable feature of the corporate bond and make the bond instead convertible into four shares of common stock. Find the loss of value to the initial shareholders of Distress, Inc.

3. You have just bought a brand-new 2013 model Fiat Cinquecento for $10,000. The resale market value of the car is expected to either increase by 20% or decrease by 20% in every subsequent year with equal probability. The car dealer also offered you a free abandonment option to sell the vehicle back to them for $8,000 at any point in time during the next 2 years. Determine whether and/or when you will optimally exercise this abandonment option.

4. You can insulate your house at a cost of $5,000. The expected savings to your electricity bill are going to be either $2,000 per year in perpetuity or $0 per year in perpetuity. From today's point of view, the probability of either event is 50%. However, by waiting 1 year,

you will find out the expected value of the savings with certainty. Your opportunity cost of capital is 25%. Find out the value today of the option to wait before deciding whether to proceed with insulating your house next year.

5. RealOption, Inc. has identified a project that will cost $100,000 to invest in. The expected free cash flows to the firm are going to be either $27,500 per year in perpetuity or $12,500 per year in perpetuity. From today's point of view, the probability of either event is 50%. However, by waiting 1 year, the firm will find out the expected value of the cash flows with certainty. The opportunity cost of capital for RealOption, Inc. is 20%. Find the value today of the option to wait before committing to a course of action next year.

6
Fixed Income Securities

Fixed income securities have historically provided a finite or an infinite stream of a constant periodic payment. They are essentially an obligation on part of the issuer to continue making the periodic payment in good faith. Typically, these were and are to this day issued by sovereign entities and, more recently, by corporations. Over time, these instruments have evolved and many of them no longer provide a fixed periodic payment per se but a floating payment that is tied to the prevailing level of interest rates. More exotic variants exist which make the periodic payment vary inversely with the general level of interest rates. In the case of fixed income securities issued by a sovereign entity denominated in local currency, these securities are considered "risk-free" in the sense that the sovereign entity can always either increase its local currency money supply or raise more money via additional taxes with which to cover its obligation. Nonsovereign issuers do not have this luxury and have to generate extra earnings or sell valuable assets in order to meet their obligations or default giving risk to credit risk. Occasionally, a sovereign issuer will denominate its bonds in a currency other than its own which also raises the issue of credit risk via its potential inability to raise sufficient foreign exchange with which to meet its foreign currency obligations.

6.1   Bond Characteristics

A bond generally has several key characteristics. These include a face value, a periodic coupon, a prespecified maturity, and a number of indentures. These latter effectively limit what the issuer is allowed to do with the funds obtained from the bondholder. In addition, for

Table 6.1 US Treasury STRIPS

Issue	Price	YTM (%)
US Treasury Stripped Int. Pmt. 15-Aug-2009	99.95	0.069
US Treasury Stripped Int. Pmt. 15-Nov-2009	99.73	0.280
US Treasury Stripped Int. Pmt. 15-Feb-2010	99.42	0.486
US Treasury Stripped Int. Pmt. 15-May-2010	99.30	0.486
US Treasury Stripped Int. Pmt. 15-Aug-2010	98.84	0.685
US Treasury Stripped Int. Pmt. 15-Nov-2010	98.67	0.686
US Treasury Stripped Prin. Pmt. 15-Feb-2011	98.65	0.615
US Treasury Stripped Int. Pmt. 15-Feb-2011	97.98	0.926
US Treasury Stripped Int. Pmt. 15-May-2011	98.00	0.826
US Treasury Stripped Prin. Pmt. 15-Aug-2011	98.59	0.525
US Treasury Stripped Int. Pmt. 15-Aug-2011	98.19	0.675
US Treasury Stripped Int. Pmt. 15-Nov-2011	97.34	0.915
US Treasury Stripped Prin. Pmt. 15-Feb-2012	97.39	0.825
US Treasury Stripped Int. Pmt. 15-Feb-2012	95.92	1.306
US Treasury Stripped Int. Pmt. 15-May-2012	95.24	1.416
⋮	⋮	⋮
US Treasury Stripped Int. Pmt. 15-Feb-2032	43.39	3.630
US Treasury Stripped Int. Pmt. 15-Feb-2033	43.59	3.460
US Treasury Stripped Int. Pmt. 15-Feb-2035	39.97	3.530
US Treasury Stripped Prin. Pmt. 15-Feb-2036	39.43	3.450
US Treasury Stripped Prin. Pmt. 15-Feb-2037	39.95	3.280
US Treasury Stripped Prin. Pmt. 15-May-2037	39.07	3.330
US Treasury Stripped Int. Pmt. 15-May-2037	38.53	3.380
US Treasury Stripped Prin. Pmt. 15-Feb-2038	39.23	3.230

Source: ValuBond.com via http://finance.yahoo.com on November 30, 2008.

corporate issuers, there may be some hurdle rates specified that the issuer needs to maintain in order to keep the bond in good standing.

Before we discuss the issue of credit risk, let us first investigate default-free securities. Table 6.1 reports information about a set of US STRIPS or zero-coupon US government bonds as of November 30, 2008.

Table 6.2 presents data on US Treasury notes and bonds as of November 30, 2008.

Table 6.3 presents details about a selected set of corporate bonds issued by US corporations as of November 30, 2008.

Occasionally, corporate bonds will have a schedule of call dates and call prices when the issuing corporation has the right to effectively prepay the corporate bond. Typically, there will be an initial call

Table 6.2   Prices of US Treasury notes and bonds

Issue	Price	Yield (%)
T-Note 3.875 15-Jan-2009	98.90	3.918
T-Note 4.750 28-Feb-2009	101.16	4.695
T-Note 2.625 15-Mar-2009	100.75	2.605
T-Note 4.500 31-Mar-2009	101.46	4.435
T-Note 3.125 15-Apr-2009	101.06	3.092
T-Note 4.500 30-Apr-2009	101.74	4.423
T-Note 5.500 15-May-2009	102.27	5.377
T-Note 3.875 15-May-2009	101.57	3.815
T-Note 4.875 15-May-2009	102.01	4.778
T-Note 4.875 31-May-2009	102.15	4.772
T-Note 4.000 15-Jun-2009	101.83	3.928
T-Note 4.875 30-Jun-2009	102.46	4.758
T-Note 3.625 15-Jul-2009	101.85	3.559
T-Note 4.625 31-Jul-2009	102.58	4.508
T-Note 6.000 15-Aug-2009	103.64	5.789
⋮	⋮	⋮
T-Bond 6.250 15-May-2030	137.94	4.531
T-Bond 5.375 15-Feb-2031	125.53	4.281
T-Bond 3.375 15-Apr-2032	108.88	3.099
T-Bond 4.500 15-Feb-2036	117.25	3.837
T-Bond 4.750 15-Feb-2037	122.81	3.867
T-Bond 5.000 15-May-2037	127.43	3.923
T-Bond 4.375 15-Feb-2038	117.19	3.733
T-Bond 4.500 15-May-2038	119.60	3.762

Source: ValuBond.com via http://finance.yahoo.com on November 30, 2008.

protection period of a few years where the bondholder can rest assured that the bond will not be called. The starting call price is typically par value plus one coupon payment and decreases as the time to maturity is neared. At the maturity of the bond the last call price is essentially the face value of the bond. This kind of feature is useful to corporate bond issuers in case interest rates decline in the future and they will be able to refinance the bond. The callable bond feature is effectively an option to prepay the loan before its maturity. This is a valuable option and as a result the callable bond will trade at a slightly lower price than an otherwise equivalent noncallable bond. Note that the notion of a yield to maturity is not very meaningful for callable bonds. Instead, practitioners frequently calculate the yield to first call or the yield to worst (YTW).

Table 6.3 Corporate bonds

Issue	Price	Coupon (%)	Maturity	Yield (%)	Fitch rating	Callable
Dow Chem Co	102.10	5.750	15-Dec-2008	5.632	A	No
General Mtrs Accep Corp	101.00	4.500	15-Dec-2008	4.455	CC	No
General Mtrs Accep Corp	101.00	4.500	15-Dec-2008	4.455	CC	No
Household Fin Corp	102.00	4.125	15-Dec-2008	4.044	AA	No
Wachovia Corp	102.02	5.625	15-Dec-2008	5.514	A	No
Ford Motor Credit Co LLC	94.75	5.800	12-Jan-2009	6.121	B	No
GMAC LLC	87.00	5.850	14-Jan-2009	6.724	CC	No
Federal Natl Mtg Assn	102.44	5.250	15-Jan-2009	5.125	AAA	No
Goldman Sachs Group Inc	102.00	3.875	15-Jan-2009	3.799	AA	No
Istar Finl Inc	98.87	4.875	15-Jan-2009	4.931	BBB	No
Morgan JP & Co Inc	102.25	6.250	15-Jan-2009	6.112	AA	No
Morgan JP & Co Inc MTN BE	102.12	6.000	15-Jan-2009	5.875	AA	No
Westdeutsche Landesbank NY BRH	101.85	6.050	15-Jan-2009	5.940	AA	No
Xerox Corp	103.00	9.750	15-Jan-2009	9.466	BBB	No
Usec Inc	100.75	6.750	20-Jan-2009	6.700	CCC	No
⋮	⋮	⋮	⋮	⋮	⋮	⋮
Kraft Foods Inc	100.58	6.875	26-Jan-2039	6.835	BBB	No
Verizon Communications Inc	108.30	8.950	1-Mar-2039	8.264	A	No
Georgia Pwr Co	91.27	6.000	1-Sep-2040	6.574	A	Yes
Georgia Pwr Co	86.80	5.650	15-Dec-2040	6.509	A	Yes
Tennessee Valley Auth	119.75	8.250	15-Apr-2042	6.889	AAA	Yes
Texaco Capital Inc	114.00	7.500	1-Mar-2043	6.579	AA	Yes
Ford Motor Co Del	23.00	7.750	15-Jun-2043	33.696	CCC	No
Pacific Bell	88.25	7.375	15-Jul-2043	8.357	A	Yes
US West Communications Inc	63.00	7.125	15-Nov-2043	11.310	BBB	Yes
Wells Fargo Capital XV	102.50	9.750	26-Sep-2044	9.512	AA	Yes
Ford Motor Co Del	26.00	7.400	1-Nov-2046	28.462	CCC	No
Ford Motor Co Del	34.00	9.980	15-Feb-2047	29.353	CCC	No
General Mtrs Corp	29.00	7.375	23-May-2048	25.431	CCC	Yes
JP Morgan Chase Cap XXII	77.00	6.450	15-Jan-2087	8.377	AA	Yes
Columbia/HCA Healthcare Corp	64.00	7.500	15-Nov-2095	11.719	B	No

Source: ValuBond.com via http://finance.yahoo.com on November 30, 2008.

Sometimes, a bond will be puttable where the option will now rest with the bondholder. Puttable bonds allow the bondholder to demand an early payment by the issuer. This is very useful in times when market interest rates increase sharply. When this happens and bondholders demand an early payment of the puttable bond, they are able to reinvest their money at higher interest rates.

One way to avoid the wild swings in coupon bond values is to make coupon rate floating and tied to the prevailing level of interest rates. This has the advantage of protecting the value of the bond. However, it has the disadvantage that when interest rates are low then the coupon payments will be low as well. Such type of bonds are generally referred to as floating rate notes or FRNs. Their coupons are tied to an index like LIBOR or EURIBOR and generally involve a fixed spread over the interest rate index to reflect a fair compensation for the perceived credit risk. An alternative to direct floating FRN are the so-called reverse or inverse floaters. These securities have coupons that vary inversely with market interest rates (e.g., LIBOR). An example of such an inverse floating coupon will be a coupon equal to $\max(10\% - \text{LIBOR}, 0)$. Note that in this particular case, if LIBOR exceeds 10% the bondholder will receive nothing. Only when LIBOR goes below 10% before the inverse floater matures the bondholder will receive some positive cash flows.

All of the previous examples suffer from one downside of all fixed income securities, namely, they do not offer any upside. One alternative that offers an upside to bondholders is the convertible bond. These are usually convertible at the option of the bondholder into a fixed number of shares of common stock of the issuing corporation. As a result of this, the issuer does not have to offer a very attractive coupon and, typically, convertible bonds pay lower coupons than otherwise equivalent nonconvertible bonds.

Turning to other hybrid securities that have both equity and fixed income characteristics leads to a brief discussion of preferred stock. These behave like fixed income securities for most intents and purposes. They pay either a fixed or a floating dividend that acts like a coupon. Preferred dividends are usually cumulative and are paid before common stock dividends. If preferred dividends are omitted over a certain period of time, preferred shareholders usually get the right to replace several board of directors members. Ironically, the biggest investors in preferred stock in the United States are corporations since they enjoy a tax advantage as only 40% of the preferred dividend is taxed. Some of the biggest issuers of preferred

Table 6.4 Inflation-indexed bond example

Time	Inflation (%)	Par value	Coupon	Principal
0		$1000		
1	2	$1020	$40.80	
2	3	$1050.60	$42.02	
3	1	$1061.11	$42.44	$1061.11

stock tend to be large financial institutions since the preferred stocks counts along with common stock in the calculation of required capital.

Other issuer of fixed income securities include state and local governments, as well as domestic corporations issuing bonds abroad and foreign corporations placing bonds in the domestic market. More recent innovations in the bond market include securitization using pools of mortgages, student loans, credit card revolver loans, car leases, etc. Some particular corporate issuers have made the coupon and, sometimes, the face value of their bonds contingent on future events. A prime example of this is the so-called catastrophe bond that is very popular with insurance companies. Catastrophe bonds typically have prespecified thresholds and number of natural disasters which, if exceeded, will suffer lower coupons and, possibly, reduced face values.

The high inflation period of the 1970s and 1980s led to the introduction of government bonds whose coupons and principals were tied to a cumulative inflation index. Such bonds are referred to as inflation indexed bonds. To illustrate how such bonds work and provide protection against inflation, we will use a simple example. Suppose we consider an inflation-protected bond promising to pay a 4% rear annual coupon with a face value of $1000 and maturing in 3 years time. Table 6.4 illustrates how the principals are continuously inflated at the realized inflation rate and the 4% coupon is applied to the inflation face value. At the maturity date of the inflation-protected bond, the bondholders receive the terminal inflation face value.

To verify that this bond indeed offers a 4% real coupon, let us calculate the nominal and real return to a bondholder from holding this bond between $t = 0$ and $t = 1$:

$$\text{Nominal return} = \frac{\text{Interest} + \text{Capital gain}}{\text{Initial price}}$$

$$= \frac{40.80 + 20}{1000} = 0.0608 \quad \text{or} \quad 6.08\%.$$

Let us verify that the real rate of return is indeed equal to 4%:

$$\text{Real return} = \frac{1 + \text{Nominal return}}{1 + \text{Inflation}} - 1$$

$$= \frac{1.0608}{1.02} - 1 = 0.04 \quad \text{or} \quad 4\%.$$

6.2 Bond Pricing

6.2.1 Basics

A fixed-coupon C finite-maturity T bond will have a present value today at $t = 0$ of

$$V_0 = \frac{C}{r}\left(1 - \frac{1}{(1+r)^T}\right) + \frac{\text{FV}}{(1+r)^T}.$$

Note that this formula uses the constant-level annuity and the present value relations from Chapter 1.

Figure 6.1 plots the present value of a fixed-coupon bond with an annual coupon of 5% and 30 years to maturity. Note that the value is

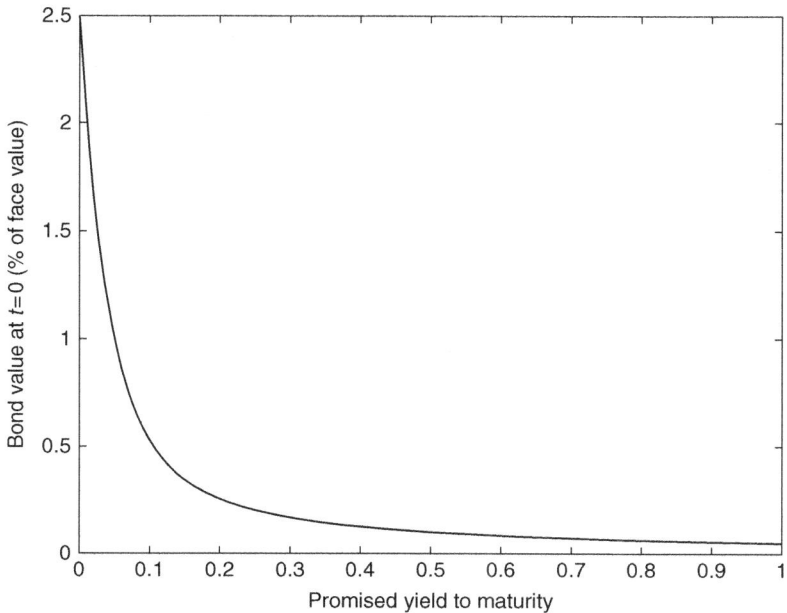

Figure 6.1   Value of fixed-coupon bond against yield to maturity.

inversely related to the yield to maturity. Bonds with higher coupons or longer tenors will plot above the one depicted.

A zero-coupon bond with a finite maturity has $C = 0$ and present value of

$$V_0 = \frac{FV}{(1+r)^T}. \tag{6.1}$$

Figure 6.2 plots the present value of a zero-coupon bond maturing in 30 years. Note that the bond value is once again inversely related to the yield to maturity.

A fixed-coupon perpetual bond value is given by

$$P_0 = \frac{C}{r}. \tag{6.2}$$

Figure 6.3 plots the present value of a fixed-coupon bond with an annual coupon of 50% paid in perpetuity. Note that the value is inversely related to the yield to maturity. Perpetual bonds with higher coupons will plot above the one depicted. Note also that in

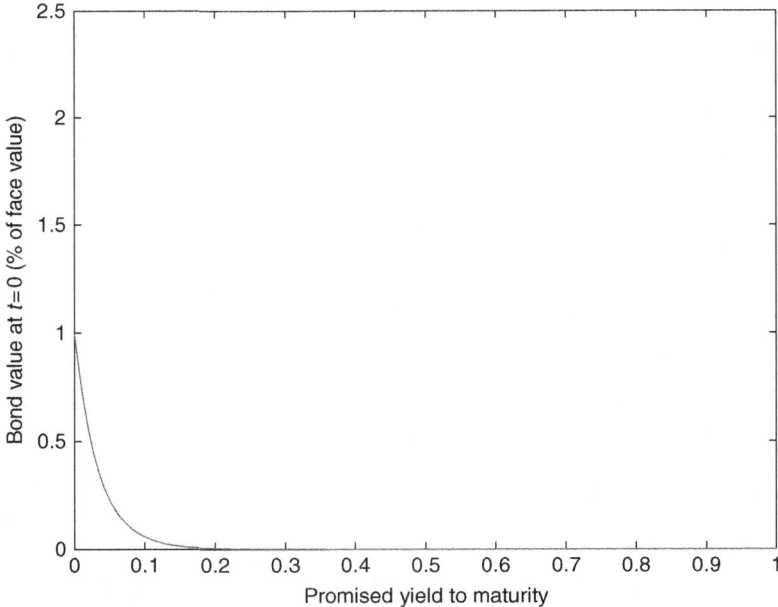

Figure 6.2   Value of zero-coupon bond against yield to maturity.

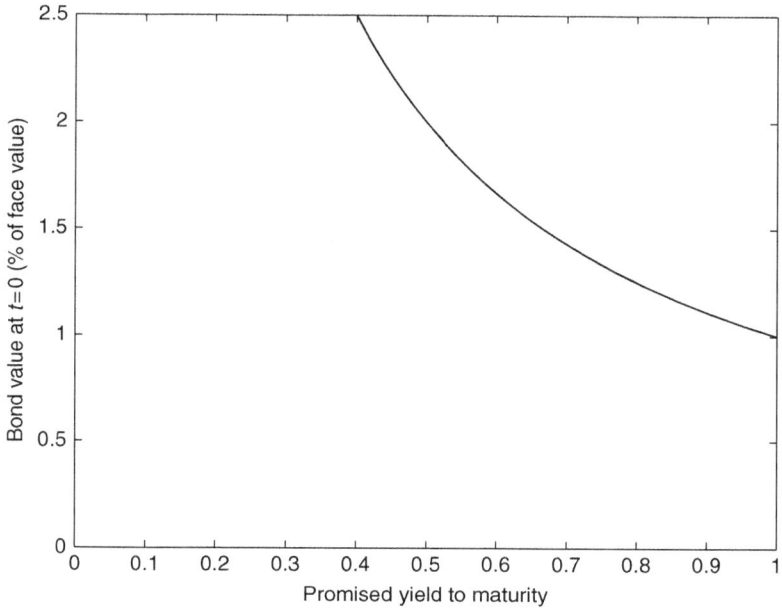

Figure 6.3   Value of perpetual bond against yield to maturity.

this case the face value is never paid back. Instead, the entire present value consists of the present value of the infinite stream of steady coupons.

6.2.2   Bond Pricing Example

Let us consider how we can price a 30-year bond with a fixed 8% coupon payed semiannually and a face value of $1000 when the current yield to maturity is 8%:

$$P_0 = \sum_{t=1}^{t=60} \frac{40}{(1.04)^t} + \frac{1000}{(1.04)^{60}} = 1000.$$

Suppose that the yield to maturity was to increase to 10% (5% for 6 months):

$$P_0 = \sum_{t=1}^{t=60} \frac{40}{(1.05)^t} + \frac{1000}{(1.05)^{60}} = 810.71.$$

Table 6.5 Bond values, time to maturity, and yield to maturity

TTM (years)	YTM (%)				
	4	6	8	10	12
1	1038.83	1029.13	1000.00	981.41	963.33
10	1327.03	1148.77	1000.00	875.35	770.60
20	1547.11	1231.15	1000.00	828.41	699.07
30	1695.22	1276.76	1000.00	810.71	676.77

6.2.3 Bond Prices at Different Times to Maturity and YTMs

Table 6.5 presents the value of a fixed 8%-coupon bond with various times to maturity and yields to maturity:

From the bond valuation formula and the above example, a few notable points emerge. First, when the yield to maturity is equal to the bond coupon rate, the bond will be selling at par value or, which is the same, the face value of the bond. Second, when the yield to maturity exceeds the coupon rate, the bond will be trading at a discount from its face value. Thirdly, if the yield to maturity is less than the bond coupon rate, the bond will be selling at a premium to face value. Finally, both the discount and the premium increase as the time to maturity increases.

6.2.4 Bond Yields

In order to find out the promised yield to maturity of a bond, we need to determine the internal rate of return (IRR) taking the cash flows as certain. Here is an example with a 30-year fixed 8%-coupon bond currently trading at 1276.76 in the marketplace:

$$1276.76 = \sum_{t=1}^{t=60} \frac{40}{(1+r)^t} + \frac{1000}{(1+r)^{60}}.$$

Solving for the IRR of these cash flows, we obtain $r = 0.03$ per half-year or 6% on a bond-equivalent yield (BEY).

Figure 6.4 plots the yield curve of US STRIPS zero-coupon bonds prevailing at the close of business on July 20, 2010. Note how the yield to maturity steadily increases and then levels off as time to maturity increases.

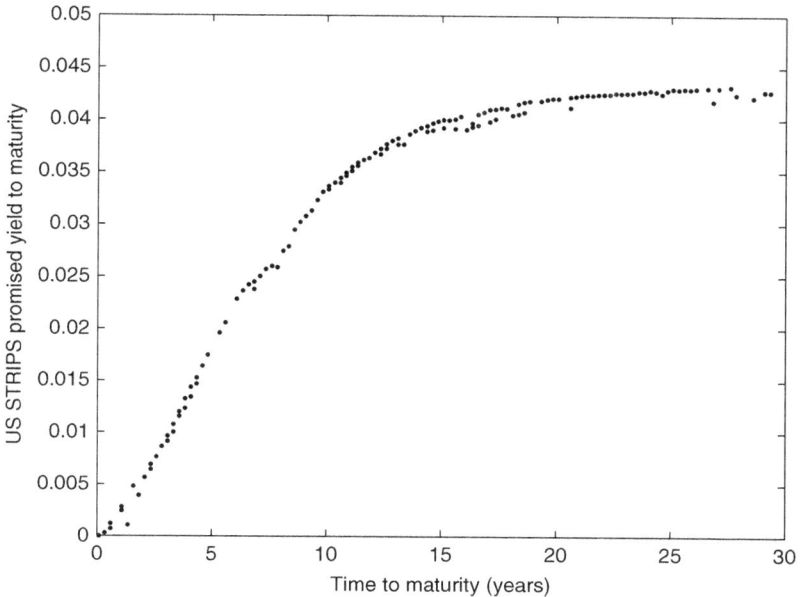

Figure 6.4   Yield curve of US STRIPS.

Figure 6.5 plots the yield curve of US Treasury bonds prevailing at the close of business on July 20, 2010. The picture is quite similar to the one for zero-coupon STRIPS and illustrates that longer maturities attract higher annualized yields.

6.2.5   Bond Yields on Callable Bonds

In order to illustrate the complications arising from yield calculations for callable bonds, it is instructive to consider a simple example. Consider a callable bond with 30 years to maturity, 8% fixed coupon paid semiannually, a face value of $1000, callable in 10 years at a call price of $1100. This bond is currently selling in the marketplace for $1150. Assuming at first that this bond is never called by the issuer, we can calculate the promised yield to maturity as follows:

$$1150 = \sum_{t=1}^{t=60} \frac{40}{(1+r)^t} + \frac{1000}{(1+r)^{60}} \quad \text{or} \quad 6.82\% \text{ BEY.}$$

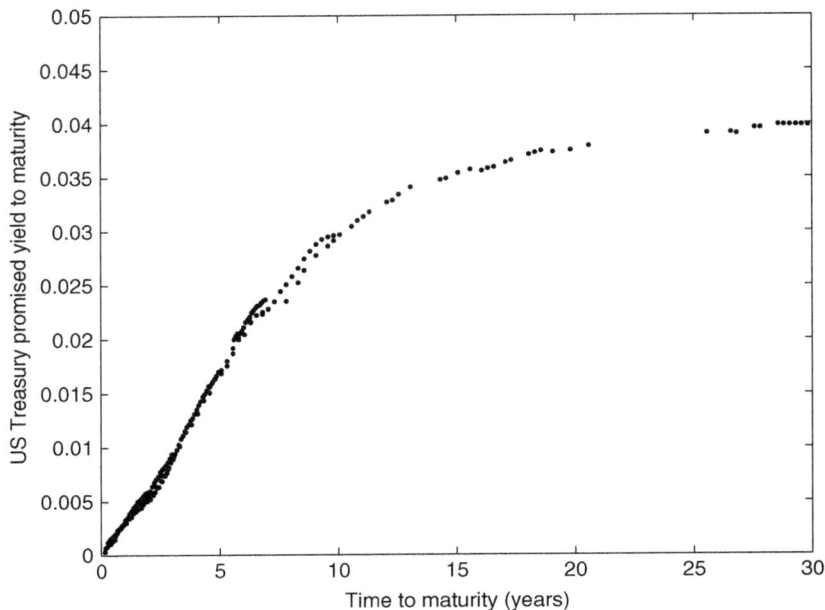

Figure 6.5   Yield curve of US Treasury notes and bonds.

Next, we calculate the yield to call (YTC) assuming that the bond will be called in 10 years at the call price of $1100:

$$1150 = \sum_{t=1}^{t=20} \frac{40}{(1+r)^t} + \frac{1100}{(1+r)^{20}} \quad \text{or} \quad 6.64\% \text{ BEY.}$$

Typically, callable bonds will have a long schedule of future call dates and call prices. One would then have to calculate the YTC for every call date. Sometimes, the worst possible YTC is reported as the YTW as the lowest value from among all the YTC values of the callable bond.

6.2.6 Credit Risk

Corporate bonds typically involve credit risk in the sense that some of the future coupons and, possibly, a portion of the face value at maturity may not be paid back in full. Table 6.6 presents an example with a risky 30-year corporate bond with a face value of $1000 and a

Table 6.6   Risky corporate bond example

	Expected YTM	Promised YTM
Coupon payment	$45	$45
Number of coupons	20	20
Final payment	$700	$1000
Price	$750	$750

9% fixed coupon paid semiannually. In order to illustrate the problem of partial recovery, we have assume a recovery rate of 70% at the maturity of the corporate bond, i.e., bondholders will receive only 70 cents on the dollar when the corporate bond matures.

We can also calculate the promised as well as the expected yield to maturity. The promised yield to maturity is 13.7% while the expected yield to maturity is only 11.6% on a BEY basis. Note that this difference is effectively a default premium reflecting the credit risk implicit in the 70% recovery rate at maturity. More complicated examples involving coupons in arrears and workouts are possible. Note that any deferment of bond cash flows into the future only serves to lower the expected as well as the promised yield to maturity of the bond. Forecasting even lower recovery rates will tend to lower the expected yield to maturity even further but will generally leave the promised yield to maturity unchanged.

6.3   Spot and Forward Interest Rates

6.3.1   The Yield Curve

In practice, the concept of an interest rate and yield to maturity needs to be clarified even further. For example, the yield of a zero-coupon bond with a certain time to maturity can be quite different from the yield to maturity of a nonzero-coupon bond with the same time to maturity. For our purposes we will need to define more formally the zero-coupon spot interest rate and the related forward interest rate. To distinguish these concept from the current value of the interest rate, we will refer to the latter as the current short rate. The zero-coupon yield curve will then be simply a plot of the zero-coupon spot rates against the respective times to maturity.

Let us denote the zero-coupon spot interest rate as y_t, where t is the future maturity date. This is an effective reinvestment risk-free rate for investing between today and time period t. Furthermore, let us define the forward interest rate as $f_{s,t}$, where the understanding is that $s \le t$. The forward interest rate is the implicit reinvestment rate that is implied in the zero-coupon spot rates. It is the per period rate at which you can reinvest money starting at a future point in time s and getting your money back even further out at time period t where $(t \ge s)$.

The explicit relationship between the zero-coupon spot interest rates and the forward interest rates can be illustrated by the following thought experiment. Consider starting with \$1 which can be invested in the 1-year zero-coupon bond at y_1 and then reinvested the forward interest rate $f_{1,2}$. Alternatively, we could invest our \$1 in the 2-year zero-coupon bond at y_2. The forward interest rate $f_{1,2}$ is the forward reinvestment rate that leads to the same amount at $t = 2$ following either of these two investment strategies. More generally, we can extend this though experiment over consecutive future time periods leading to the following:

$$(1 + f_{0,1}) = (1 + y_1),$$
$$(1 + y_1)(1 + f_{1,2}) = (1 + y_2)^2,$$
$$(1 + y_2)^2(1 + f_{2,3}) = (1 + y_3)^3,$$

$$\vdots \quad \vdots \quad \vdots$$

$$(1 + y_{t-1})^{t-1}(1 + f_{t-1,t}) = (1 + y_t)^t.$$

The existence of nominal unit of account in the form of universally acceptable currency leads to the following requirements on the zero-coupon and forward risk-free interest rates in order to avoid arbitrage:

$$y_t \ge 0 \quad \forall t,$$
$$f_{s,t} \ge 0 \quad \forall s \le t.$$

The proof of these is quite simple and it has to do with the fact that the nominal rate of return on cash is 0. Hence, we would never invest or reinvest at a negative zero-coupon or forward interest rate since we would be better off selling them and keeping our money in cash.

6.4   Term Structure of Interest Rates

Economists have developed several theories about the term structure of interest rates. The following discussion is only meant to cover the basic ideas and the intuition behind the main term structure theories without getting bogged down into too much detail.

6.4.1   Expectations Hypothesis

The expectations hypothesis states that our best guess today at tomorrow's short rate is the forward interest rate we can observe today built into the zero-coupon spot interest rates coming from zero-coupon bonds. Mathematically, this means the following:

$$E(r_2) = f_{1,2}$$
$$(1 + y_2)^2 = (1 + r_1)(1 + f_{1,2})$$
$$= (1 + r_1)(1 + E(r_2)).$$

If this hypothesis is true, it implies that we do not need liquidity premia on long-term bonds in order to induce bondholders to roll over their holdings at the then prevailing future short interest rate.

6.4.2   Liquidity Preference

The liquidity preference theory maintains that the expected future short rates are not necessarily equal to the forward interest rates and are typically less:

$$E(r_2) \neq f_{1,2}$$
$$E(r_2) < f_{1,2} \quad \text{typically}$$

The logic behind this is that investors prefer to invest in more liquid bonds with shorter maturities. In order for investors to be induced to hold less liquid bonds with longer maturities, they will have to be compensated with a liquidity premium built into the promised yield to maturity. This will typically be reflected in a liquidity discount in the bond price.

6.4.3   Market Segmentation

The market segmentation theory states that short-maturity and long-maturity bonds trade in essentially separate markets with different investors sticking to their preferred maturities. No amount of price discounting or premia can induce a long-maturity investor to cross over and invest in a short-maturity bond. Vice versa, a short-maturity investor will never be induced to switch over and acquire a long-maturity bond. This theory is not very popular nowadays. The reason for this is that there are finite amounts of yield premia and discounts that will persuade a bondholder to acquire them regardless of his or her preferred maturity.

6.4.4 Preferred Habitat Theories

The preferred habitat theory is a modified and less extreme version of the segmented markets theory. It postulates that bond investors compare short-maturity and long-maturity bonds while having a certain preference for one or the other. However, bond investors may be induced to cross over from their preferred maturity "habitat" into another one for the right price.

6.4.5 Interpreting the Term Structure

One way these theories can be useful is to try and base forecasts about expected future short rates on the forward risk-free interest rates. Sometimes, we can assume that there are constant liquidity premia for every maturity. More generally though, we may use maturity-specific liquidity premia as follows:

$$f_{n,n+1} = E(r_n) + \text{Liquidity premium.}$$

We can safely assume that the liquidity premia increase as the time to maturity increases. However, whether that is true or not in practice is an empirical question.

6.4.6 Measuring the Term Structure

It order to illustrate how we can use actual bond prices to measure the risk-free zero-coupon discount rates across various maturities, we will use the following simplified example. Consider a 1-year 8% fixed-coupon bond (paid semiannually) and currently trading at 986.10. Consider also another 1-year 10% fixed-coupon bond (also paid semiannually) and selling at 1004.78. We can link the future coupons and face values with the risk-free zero-coupon discount factors d_1, the present value of $1 receivable in 6 months, and d_2, the present value of $1 receivable in 12 months is as follows:

$$986.10 = d_1 \times 40 + d_2 \times 1040,$$
$$1004.78 = d_1 \times 50 + d_2 \times 1050,$$

where the solution is given by $d_1 = 0.95694$ and $d_2 = 0.91137$, which implies $y_1 = 0.045$ and $f_{1,2} = 0.05$.

6.4.7   More Bonds than Time Periods

In general, we can perform the same exercise with many bonds. However, it becomes impossible to fit all bond prices at the same time with the same rates. The reason for this is that there are typically many more bonds than there are periods until the maturity of the bonds with the longest time to maturity. Therefore, we can only fit all bonds with a certain measure of pricing error. One possible way to do this is to perform the following cross-sectional regression without any intercept:

$$P_1 = \hat{d}_1 CF_{11} + \hat{d}_2 CF_{12} + \hat{d}_3 CF_{13} + \cdots + \hat{e}_1,$$
$$P_2 = \hat{d}_1 CF_{21} + \hat{d}_2 CF_{22} + \hat{d}_3 CF_{23} + \cdots + \hat{e}_2,$$
$$P_3 = \hat{d}_1 CF_{31} + \hat{d}_2 CF_{32} + \hat{d}_3 CF_{33} + \cdots + \hat{e}_3,$$
$$\vdots \quad \vdots \quad \vdots$$
$$P_n = \hat{d}_1 CF_{n1} + \hat{d}_2 CF_{n2} + \hat{d}_3 CF_{n3} + \cdots + \hat{e}_n,$$

where P_i is the current market price of bond i, CF_{ij} is the cash flow coming from bond i in time period j, $\hat{e}_i$ is the pricing error of bond i, and $\hat{d}_t$ is the risk-free discount factor today of \$1 payable in time period t.

Note that we may have to impose the following no-arbitrage restrictions while running the above regression:

$$1 \geq \hat{d}_1 \geq \hat{d}_2 \geq \hat{d}_3 \geq \cdots \geq \hat{d}_T.$$

6.5   Fixed Income Arbitrage Strategies

Suppose we observe the following market spot interest rates: $y_1 = 0.10$ and $y_2 = 0.04$. If these were indeed market rates and you can freely borrow and lend at them, how can you make infinite profits without putting any of your own money at risk? Let us check the implied value of the forward interest rate $f_{1,2}$:

$$f_{1,2} = \frac{(1 + y_2)^2}{(1 + y_1)} - 1$$

$$= \frac{(1.04)^2}{(1.10)} - 1$$

$$= -0.0167 \quad \text{or} \quad -1.67\%.$$

But holding our money in cash (at a zero nominal rate of return) dominates rolling over our investment forward between time periods 1 and 2 (at a negative forward interest rate). Here are the arbitrage trade steps. First, we borrow \$1 for 2 years at $y_2 = 0.04$ by selling short a two-period zero-coupon bond, for example. We have to pay back \$1.0816 at $t = 2$. Second, we invest \$1 for one period at the one-period spot interest rate $y_1 = 0.10$ by buying a 1-year zero-coupon bond. At $t = 1$, we have \$1.10 which we liquidate after the one-period zero-coupon bond matures and hold the money in cash until $t = 2$. Finally, at $t = 2$ we pay back our debt of \$1.0816. This leaves us with an arbitrage profit of \$0.0184 per \$1 borrowed at $t = 0$.

Let us consider another fixed income arbitrage trade involving two bonds maturing at the same time. Suppose we observe the following risk-free market spot rates $y_1 = y_2 = 0.20$. We also observe one risk-free government 20%-coupon bond with a face value of \$1000, 2 years to maturity, that is trading at par (\$1000) on the market (assume annual coupons payments). There is another two-year risk-free government zero-coupon bond with a face value of \$1000 and 2 years to maturity which is currently trading at \$833.33. Purchasing either one of these two bonds at $t = 0$ results in the following cash flows:

Bond	$t = 0$	$t = 1$	$t = 2$
20%-coupon	−1000	+200	+1200
Zero-coupon	−833.33	0	+1000

First, let us compute the implied spot 2-year interest rate y_2^{implied}:

$$y_2^{\text{implied}} = \sqrt{\frac{1000}{833.33}} - 1 = 0.0954 \quad \text{or} \quad 9.54\%.$$

This rate is much smaller than the market spot rate $y_2 = 0.20$. We should borrow at this implied rate while investing at the higher market rate at the same time. Let us sell short 12 zeros and buy 10

20%-coupon bonds with the proceeds from the short sale. This results in the following cash flows:

Arbitrage strategy	$t=0$	$t=1$	$t=2$
Buy 10 20%, Sell 12 zeros	0	+2000	0

More generally, let us consider the case of two risk-free bonds, A and B, with the same maturity T, with prices, p_A and p_B, and coupons, c_A and c_B, expressed as percent of their respective face values. We know that the following need to hold based on simple present value relations:

$$p_A = c_A \left(\sum_{t=1}^{t=T} d_t \right) + d_T, \tag{6.3}$$

$$p_B = c_B \left(\sum_{t=1}^{t=T} d_t \right) + d_T. \tag{6.4}$$

It is straightforward to show that the risk-free present T-annuity factor and the risk-free discount factor d_T are given by

$$\sum_{t=1}^{t=T} d_t = \left(\frac{p_A - p_B}{c_A - c_B} \right), \tag{6.5}$$

$$d_T = \left(\frac{c_A p_B - c_B p_A}{c_A - c_B} \right). \tag{6.6}$$

Once again, the presence of a monetary unit of account puts a constraint on the pattern of risk-free discount factors as the time to maturity increases. The above two values have to satisfy the following constraints:

$$0 < \sum_{t=1}^{t=T} d_t \leq T, \tag{6.7}$$

$$0 < d_T \leq 1, \tag{6.8}$$

$$T \leq \frac{\sum_{t=1}^{t=T} d_t}{d_T}. \tag{6.9}$$

First, it it obvious that if the bonds have the same coupon rates, i.e., $c_A = c_B$, then they have to have the same prices, $p_A = p_B$. Second, to eliminate this uninteresting case let us assume without loss of generality that $c_A > c_B$. Then it is easy to express the above constraints in terms of the coupon rates and bond prices as follows:

$$p_A > p_B, \quad \text{if } c_A > c_B, \tag{6.10}$$

$$\frac{p_A - p_B}{c_A - c_B} \le T, \tag{6.11}$$

$$\frac{p_A}{p_B} < \frac{c_A}{c_B} \le \left(\frac{p_A - 1}{p_B - 1}\right), \tag{6.12}$$

$$\frac{p_A}{p_B} \ge \left(\frac{1 + T c_A}{1 + T c_B}\right). \tag{6.13}$$

Next, let us consider a more involved fixed income arbitrage example using three bonds maturing at the same time. Suppose we observe the following market prices for three risk-free government bond that pay annual coupons and have 3 years remaining to maturity:

Bond	Maturity	Coupon	Price	Face Value
A	3	0%	$751.30	$1000.00
E	3	14%	$1120.12	$1000.00
F	3	7%	$1001.62	$1000.00

This means that purchasing any of the above bonds will result in the following cash flows:

Bond	$t = 0$	$t = 1$	$t = 2$	$t = 3$
A	−751.30	0	0	+1000
E	−1120.12	+140	+140	+1140
F	−1001.62	+70	+70	+1070

The magnitudes of the annual coupons already give us an idea of what to try. Suppose we buy 1 unit of bond A and 1 unit of bond E. We shall try and finance our purchases by selling short 2 units of bond F. Let us look at the resulting cash flows:

Strategy	$t=0$	$t=1$	$t=2$	$t=3$
Buy 1 A	−751.30	0	0	+1000
Buy 1 E	−1120.12	+140	+140	+1140
Sell 2F	+2003.24	−140	−140	−2140
Net Cash Flow	+131.82	0	0	0

This is a classic example of an arbitrage trade. These types of trades are the bread and butter of many fixed income hedge fund traders. This trade would also obviously work with any positive multiple, i.e., we could have bought 10 A, 10 E, and shorted 20 F bonds just as well and make 10 times more money. The trade is set up, so that we take out the profit immediately but this is not a requirement. An alternative would be to create a trade that results in one final positive cash flow at the maturity date of the bonds. Another alternative is to construct a trade resulting in a stream of positive net cash flows at every future coupon payment date.

Let us try and be a little more systematic in finding the arbitrage trade. Denote by n_A, n_E, and n_F the number of A, E, and F bonds we plan to hold, respectively. We would like our strategy to generate zero cash flows in all future periods which means there should be no net payment of principal and coupons at all future dates:

$$1000 \times n_A + 1000 \times n_E + 1000 \times n_F = 0,$$
$$0 \times n_A + 140 \times n_E + 70 \times n_F = 0.$$

Note that the system is underidentified, i.e., we have more unknowns than we have equations. But this is exactly what we would expect if there is an arbitrage present as any positive multiple of an arbitrage is also an arbitrage, i.e., generically this system will have infinitely many solutions. This feature of arbitrage trades also makes it easier to solve for them since finding one arbitrage means we have found all of them.

One way to solve this system is to express two of the unknowns in terms of the third. In this case, let us try solving for n_A and n_F in terms of n_E:

$$n_A = n_E,$$

$$n_F = -2 \times n_E.$$

All we need to do now is figure out the sign of n_E so we try either $n_E = +1$ or $n_E = -1$ as one of these makes money while the other one loses money. If our initial try loses money, we can just switch all the signs and find the arbitrage trade if it exists.

Let us try another example where all three bonds have nonzero-coupon rates. Consider the following three bonds:

Bond	Maturity	Coupon	Price	Face Value
B	4	5%	$842.30	$1000
C	4	12%	$1065.28	$1000
D	4	10%	$980.57	$1000

Purchasing either one of these bonds will result in the following cash flows:

Bond	$t = 0$	$t = 1$	$t = 2$	$t = 3$	$t = 4$
B	−842.30	+50	+50	+50	+1050
C	−1065.28	+120	+120	+120	+1120
D	−980.57	+100	+100	+100	+1100

Let us set up two equations to find the arbitrage trade resulting in profit at $t = 0$:

$$1000 \times n_B + 1000 \times n_C + 1000 \times n_D = 0,$$

$$50 \times n_B + 120 \times n_C + 100 \times n_D = 0.$$

Let us solve for n_C and n_D in terms of n_B (purely arbitrary choice):

$$n_C = 2.5 \times n_B,$$

$$n_D = -3.5 \times n_B.$$

Let us try $n_B = +1$; this means we also have $n_C = 2.5$ and $n_D = -3.5$. Conceptually, we are selling 1 unit of B and 2.5 units of C while buying 3.5 units of D:

Strategy	$t = 0$	$t = 1$	$t = 2$	$t = 3$	$t = 4$
Sell 1 B	+842.30	−50	−50	−50	−1050
Sell 2.5 C	+2663.20	−300	−300	−300	−2800
Buy 3.5 D	−3431.995	+350	+350	+350	+3850
Net cash flows	+73.305	0	0	0	0

Note that every bond that we are selling as part of the arbitrage strategy must be overvalued while every bond that we are buying as part of the arbitrage strategy must be undervalued. Gradually, arbitrageurs' activities will bring prices back to where they need to be. In practice, we may have to use cash for margin (for anything we sell short) which ties up capital—this tends to limit the scale of the arbitrage trade. A good example of this is the liquidity price differential between on-the-run and off-the-run bonds (with the same remaining time to maturity).

In general, when all three bonds have the same face values and mature at the same time, the requirement to avoid arbitrage is that the arbitrage trade solves the following system of equations:

$$c_A n_A + c_B n_B + c_C n_C = 0,$$
$$F(n_A + n_B + n_C) = 0,$$
$$P_A n_A + P_B n_B + P_C n_C = 0,$$

which simplifies to the following equation:

$$P_A(c_B - c_C) + P_B(c_C - c_A) + P_C(c_A - c_B) = 0. \qquad (6.14)$$

As soon as the above evaluates to a nonzero number, this is a sufficient condition for the existence of an arbitrage trade.

More generally, when the three bonds have different face values but still mature at the same time we have to satisfy the following set of equations:

$$c_A n_A + c_B n_B + c_C n_C = 0,$$
$$F_A n_A + F_B n_B + F_C n_C = 0,$$
$$P_A n_A + P_B n_B + P_C n_C = 0,$$

which simplifies to the following equation:

$$P_A(c_B F_C - c_C F_B) + P_B(c_C F_A - c_A F_C)$$
$$+ P_C(c_A F_B - c_B F_A) = 0. \tag{6.15}$$

Once again, as soon as the above quantity results in a nonzero number this is a sufficient condition for the existence of an arbitrage trade.

6.6   Duration

Starting again with the general present value formula for the bond today:

$$P_{\text{bond}} = \sum_{t=1}^{t=T} \text{PV}(\text{Coupon}_t) + \text{PV}(\text{Face value}_T).$$

We can define the Macaulay duration as the sensitivity of the bond value today to a small change in the yield to maturity. This leads to the following formula:

$$\text{Macaulay duration} = \sum_{t=1}^{t=T} \frac{\text{PV}(C_t)}{P_{\text{bond}}} \times t + \frac{\text{PV}(\text{FV}_T)}{P_{\text{bond}}} \times T. \tag{6.16}$$

Note that the Macaulay duration is effectively a weighted-average time to maturity where the weights are proportional to the present value today of the respective cash flows, whether they are coupons or the final face value.

Sometimes it is useful to consider a modified version of the Macaulay duration which is scaled by one plus the yield to maturity, also referred to as modified duration or bond volatility:

$$\text{Modified duration} = \frac{\text{Macaulay duration}}{1 + y}. \tag{6.17}$$

where y is the yield to maturity.

Bond duration is useful as a first-order approximation to what happens to the bond price for a small change in the yield to

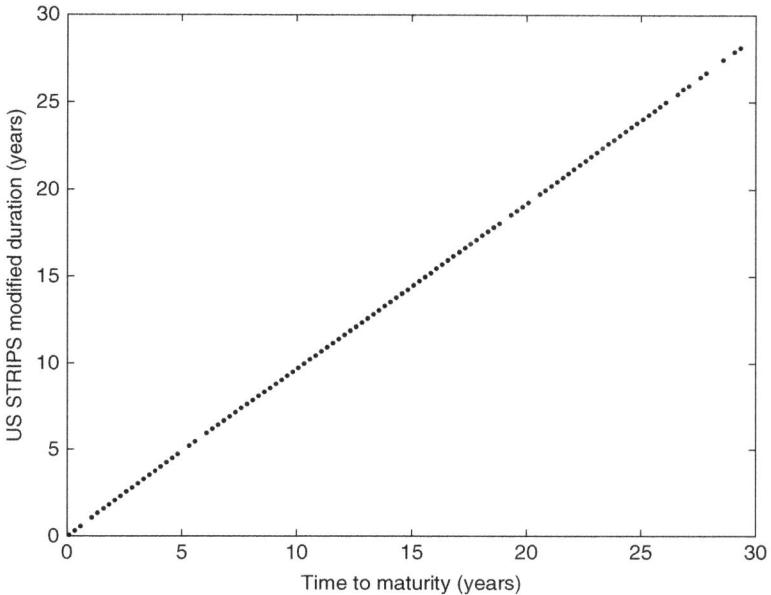

Figure 6.6   Modified duration of US STRIPS.

maturity:

$$\frac{\Delta P_{\text{bond}}}{P_{\text{bond}}} = -\text{Modified duration} \times \Delta y. \qquad (6.18)$$

Figure 6.6 plots the modified duration of US STRIPS zero-coupon bonds as of July 20, 2010.

Figure 6.7 plots the modified duration of US Treasury bonds as of July 20, 2010.

Bond duration is a measure of interest rate risk for bonds. It also varies for the same bond with the general level of interest rates. Duration is high when the yield to maturity is low. Vice versa, when the yield to maturity is high then duration is generally low, all else being equal. Note also that duration is lower the higher the coupon rate of the bond is. In the limit, when we are considering a zero-coupon bond duration is at its highest possible level for bonds with the same time to maturity. Finally, when we let the time to maturity go to infinity, duration has the absolute highest possible

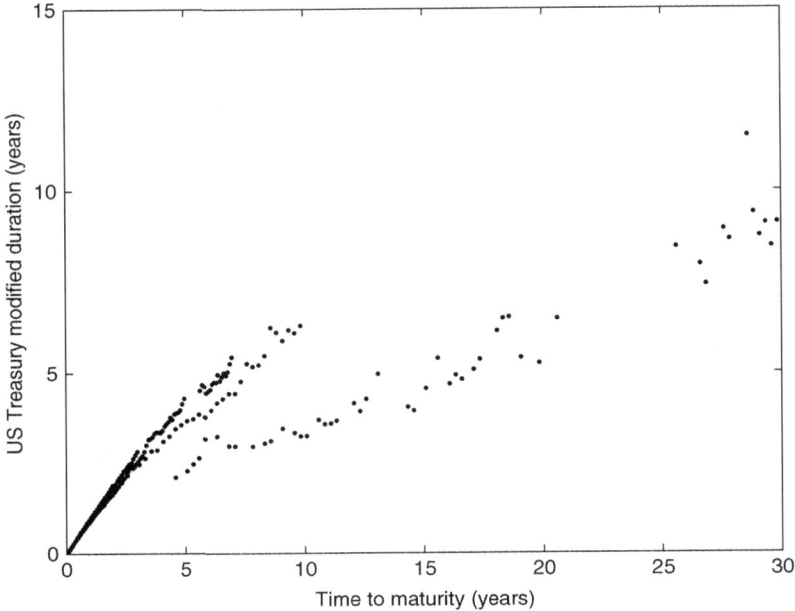

Figure 6.7 Modified duration of US Treasury notes and bonds.

value. Hence, perpetual bonds have the highest possible level of interest rate risk.

6.7 Convexity

Recall from the bond values depicted in previous sections of this chapter that the present bond value is a nonlinear convex function of the yield to maturity. Hence, a linear approximation using just the modified duration measure would be accurate only for the tiniest changes in the yield to maturity. A much more accurate approximation obtains once we consider the second-order effect to account for the curvature of the bond value with respect to the yield to maturity. This is technically the second-order derivative of the bond value with respect to the yield to maturity. This quantity is referred to as the convexity measure and is given by the following:

$$\text{Convexity} = \frac{1}{(1+y)^2} \left[\sum_{t=1}^{t=T} \frac{\text{PV}(C_t)}{P_{\text{bond}}} \times t \times (t+1) \right]$$

$$+ \frac{PV(FV_T)}{P_{bond}} \times T \times (T+1) \Bigg].\qquad (6.19)$$

Note that, once again, we have a weighted average of $t \times (t+1)$ for $t = 1,\ldots,T$. The weights are proportional to the present value of the respective cash flows, be it coupons or the face value. It is quite obvious that zero-coupon bonds will have a very large convexity measure especially those zero-coupon bonds that have a long time to maturity. Vice versa, bonds with high coupon rates will have lower convexity measures, all else being equal. The convexity measure itself depends implicitly on the yield to maturity through the present value calculations in the above formula. When the yield to maturity is low for a bond with a nonzero coupon, the convexity measure will be lower than otherwise.

Figure 6.8 plots the convexity measure of US STRIPS zero-coupon bonds as of July 20, 2010.

Figure 6.9 plots the convexity measure of US Treasury bonds as of July 20, 2010.

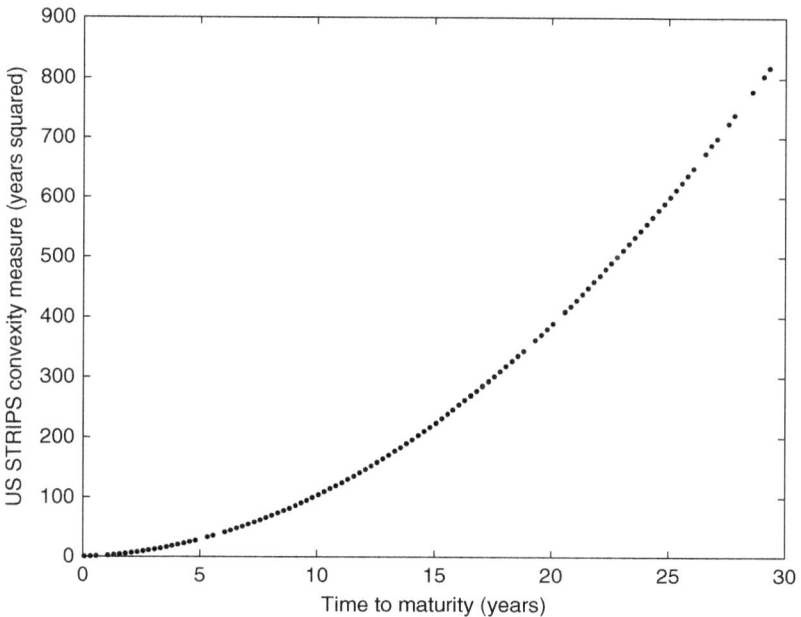

Figure 6.8   Convexity measure of US STRIPS.

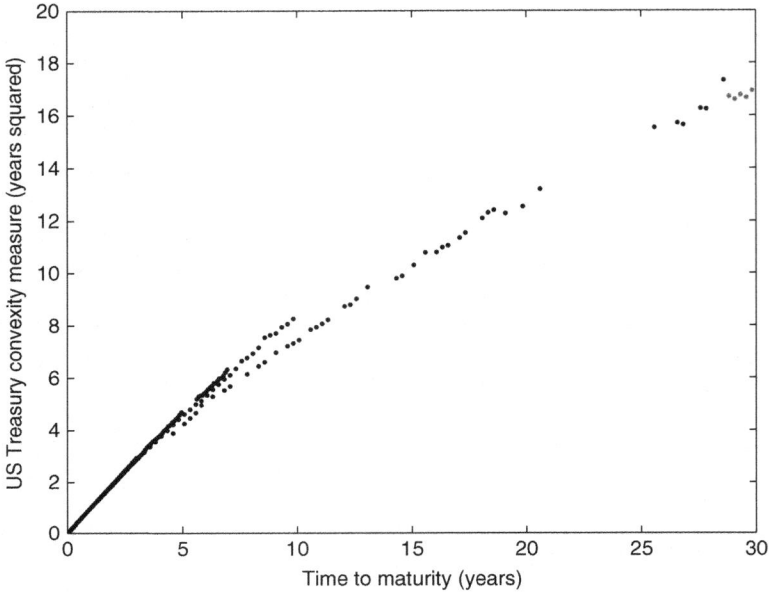

Figure 6.9   Convexity measure of US Treasury notes and bonds.

Bond convexity is useful as a second-order, and more accurate, approximation to what happens to bond prices when the yield to maturity changes by a small amount:

$$\frac{\Delta P_{\text{bond}}}{P_{\text{bond}}} = -\text{Modified duration}$$

$$\times \Delta y + \tfrac{1}{2}\text{Convexity} \times (\Delta y)^2. \tag{6.20}$$

This is essentially a second-order approximation to the percentage change in the bond value for small changes in the yield to maturity. This approximation is quite accurate locally and there seems to be not worthwhile investigating a third-order approximation. For this reason, in practice, most investors would focus on just the slope and curvature of the bond value with respect to small changes in interest rates.

6.8   Bond Portfolios

Bonds with higher duration measures contain more interest rate risk by definition. The same change in the yield to maturity will have a higher impact on the value of a bond with a higher duration measure. At the same time, bonds with higher convexity measures are preferred by bond investors. Between two bonds with equal duration measures, the one with the higher convexity measure will preserve its value better as a result of changes in interest rates than the bond with the lower convexity measure. Therefore, it is natural to think of bond duration as a measure of risk and of bond convexity as a measure of upside potential or, at least, limited downside. Furthermore, the bond portfolio problem is considerably simplified by the fact that the duration and convexity measures for a bond portfolio are simply a weighted-average linear function of the duration and convexity measures of the individual bonds that enter the portfolio.

Consider the problem of maximizing a bond portfolio's convexity subject to a target level for the modified duration of the portfolio:

$$\text{Maximize} \sum_{i=1}^{i=N} w_i \times \text{Convexity}_i$$

$$\text{Subject to} \sum_{i=1}^{i=N} w_i \times \text{Modified duration}_i = \text{Target MD}$$

$$\sum_{i=1}^{i=N} w_i = 1$$

$$w_i \geq 0, \quad \forall i = 1, \dots, N.$$

The solution to this portfolio problem is, typically, what is referred to as the bar-bell portfolio. This portfolio will consist of holdings of the bonds with the smallest and the greatest duration measures. If the investable bond universe under consideration contains only zero-coupon bonds, then the bar-bell portfolio is always the solution as can be seen by inspecting the modified duration and convexity measure formulae for zero-coupon bonds explained later.

Figure 6.10 plots the modified duration against the convexity measure for US STRIPS zero-coupon bonds as of July 20, 2010.

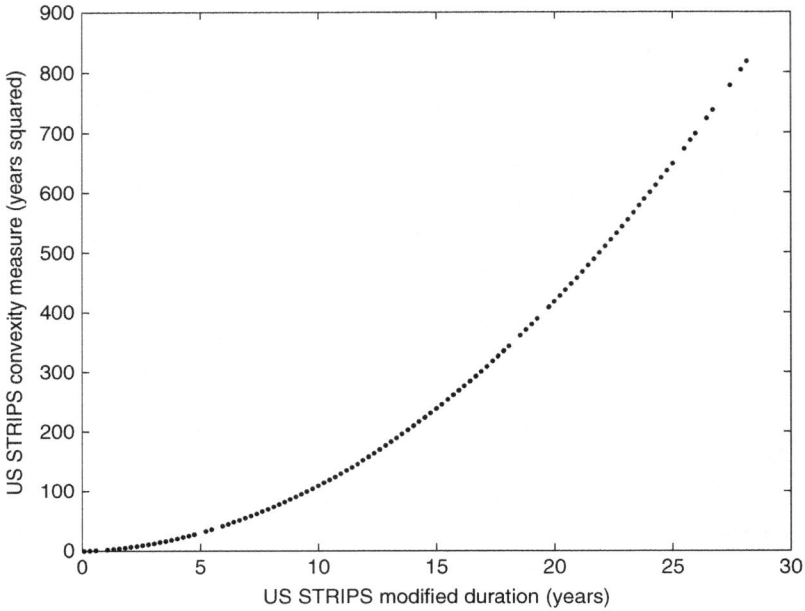

Figure 6.10 Modified duration versus convexity measure of US STRIPS.

Figure 6.11 plots the modified duration against the convexity measure for US Treasury bonds as of July 20, 2010.

The duration and convexity measures of a zero-coupon bond with T years to maturity and a yield to maturity equal to y are as follows:

Macaulay duration $= T$,

$$\text{Modified duration} = \frac{T}{1+y},$$

$$\text{Convexity} = \frac{T \times (T+1)}{(1+y)^2}.$$

A perpetual bond does not really have a yield to maturity but we can instead calculate the current yield as the ratio of the level coupon payment to the face value. A perpetual bond with a current yield of y has the following duration and convexity measures:

$$\text{Macaulay duration} = \frac{1+y}{y},$$

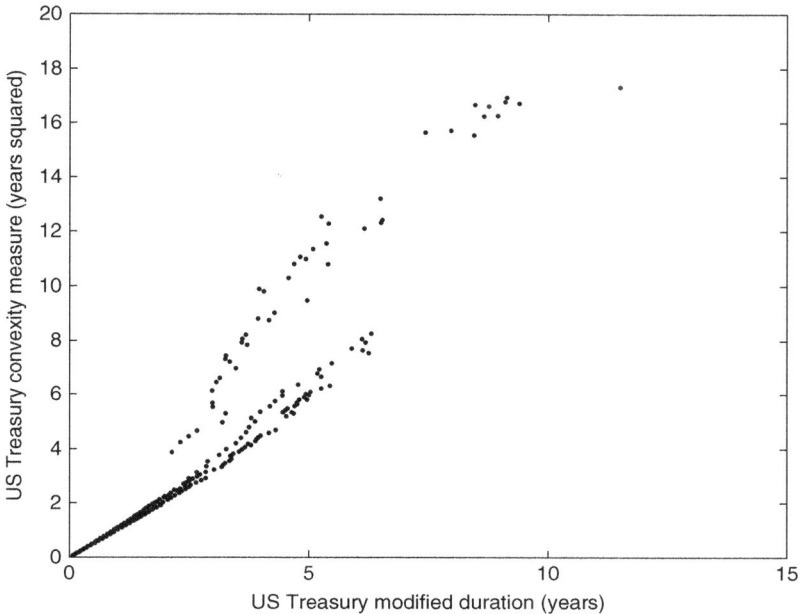

Figure 6.11   Modified duration versus convexity measure of US Treasury notes and bonds.

$$\text{Modified duration} = \frac{1}{y},$$

$$\text{Convexity} = \frac{2}{y^2}.$$

Fixed nonzero-coupon bonds with finite maturities have duration and convexity measures that are smaller than the corresponding measures for an otherwise equivalent zero-coupon bond. A fixed-coupon bond with a yield to maturity of y and a coupon rate of c has the following duration measures:

$$\text{Macaulay duration} = \frac{1+y}{y} - \frac{(1+y) + T(c-y)}{c[(1+y)^T - 1] + y},$$

$$\text{Modified duration} = \frac{\text{Macaulay duration}}{(1+y)}.$$

Note that the modified duration of the fixed-coupon bond is always less than the modified duration of the zero-coupon bond.

Problems

1. Consider the following risk-free government bonds with fixed coupons that are paid annually at the end of every year. All three coupons mature at the same time and have the same face value of 100. None of these bonds has any callable or puttable features. Assume that the time 0 zero coupon has already been paid.

Bond	Coupon (%)	Price	Face value	Time to maturity (years)
A	2	98	100	2
B	1	97	100	2

Determine which of the two bonds is overvalued and which is undervalued relative to each other.

2. Consider the following risk-free government bonds with fixed coupons that are paid annually at the end of every year. All three coupons mature at the same time and have the same face value of 100. None of these bonds has any callable or puttable features. Assume that the time 0 zero coupon has already been paid.

Bond	Coupon (%)	Price	Face value	Time to maturity (years)
A	0	45	100	10
B	3	90	100	10
C	5	120	100	10

Determine which of the bonds are undervalued and which are overvalued relative to each other.

3. Consider the following risk-free government bonds with fixed coupons that are paid annually at the end of every year. None of these bonds has any callable or puttable features. Assume that the time 0 zero coupon has already been paid. The table below reports coupons, market prices, face values, and the maturity date for each bond.

Bond	Coupon (%)	Price	Face value	Time to maturity (years)
A	0	100	100	15
B	1	99	100	15
C	2	97	100	15

After extensive research, you conclude that both bonds A and B are fairly valued. Determine whether bond C is undervalued, overvalued, or fairly valued relative to bonds A and B.

7

Fixed Income Derivatives

7.1   Interest Rate Models

7.1.1   Traditional Term Structure Models

In the following presentation of various term structure models, we shall adopt the following notation. Let $P(t,s)$ denote the price at time t of a zero-coupon bond with a face value of one that matures at time $s \geq t$. Let $R(t,s)$ denote the yield to maturity at time t of a zero-coupon bond with a face value of one maturing at time $s \geq t$. Furthermore, let $f(t,s)$ be the forward interest rate at time t for time $s \geq t$. Finally, we shall denote the volatility of the zero-coupon yield $R(t,s)$ as $\sigma_R(t,s)$.

Vasicek Model

Vasicek (1977) proposed a simple model of mean-reverting short rate where the continuous time evolution of the short rate is given by

$$dr_t = \kappa(\bar{r} - r_t)dt + \sigma\,dz, \tag{7.1}$$

where κ is the speed of mean reversion, $\bar{r}$ is long-run level of the interest rate toward which the short rate is mean reverting to, σ is the volatility of the short rate, and dz is a standard Brownian motion. As can be seen immediately from this specification, these is no guarantee that the short rate will stay strictly non-negative and a similar problem arises for forward interest rates in the Vasicek (1977) model. Nevertheless, this is perhaps the simplest interest rate model out there so it is worthwhile to consider its implications for zero-coupon bond prices, yields, and yield volatilities.

Zero-coupon bond prices maturing at $t = T$ have the following prices at $t < T$ and yields to maturity $R(t,s)$ for $s > t$:

$$P(t,s) = A(t,s)e^{-r_t B(t,s)}, \tag{7.2}$$

$$R(t,s) = -\frac{\ln A(t,s)}{s-t} + \frac{B(t,s)}{s-t}r_t, \tag{7.3}$$

where

$$B(t,s) = \frac{1}{\kappa}\left(1 - e^{-\kappa(s-t)}\right), \tag{7.4}$$

$$\ln A(t,s) = \frac{R_\infty}{\kappa}\left(1 - e^{-\kappa(s-t)}\right) - (s-t)R_\infty$$
$$-\frac{\sigma^2}{4\kappa^3}\left(1 - e^{-\kappa(s-t)}\right)^2, \tag{7.5}$$

$$R_\infty = \lim_{\tau \to \infty} R(t,\tau) = \bar{r} - \frac{1}{2}\frac{\sigma^2}{\kappa^2}. \tag{7.6}$$

The spot rate volatility is determined by the two parameters σ and κ:

$$\sigma_R(t,s) = \frac{\sigma}{\kappa(s-t)}\left(1 - e^{-\kappa(s-t)}\right), \tag{7.7}$$

and has the very desirable quality of exponential decay as the time to maturity increases, something that is often observed in the data on zero-coupon yield volatilities.

Figure 7.1 plots the zero-coupon bond prices, zero-coupon spot, and forward interest rates, as well as the spot rate volatility in a Vasicek model with parameter values $\kappa = 0.15$, $\bar{r} = 0.05$, $r_t = 0.045$, and $\sigma = 0.01$.

The other appealing feature of the Vasicek (1977) interest rate model is that it is relatively straightforward to price options on zero-coupon bonds in the context of the model with relatively simple closed-form formulae resembling the Black and Scholes (1973) equity option pricing model. Jamshidian (1989) has shown that under the process (7.1), European discount bond call and put option prices are given by

$$c(t,T,s) = P(t,s)N(d_1) - KP(t,T)N(d_2), \tag{7.8}$$

$$p(t,T,s) = KP(t,T)N(-d_2) - P(t,s)N(-d_1), \tag{7.9}$$

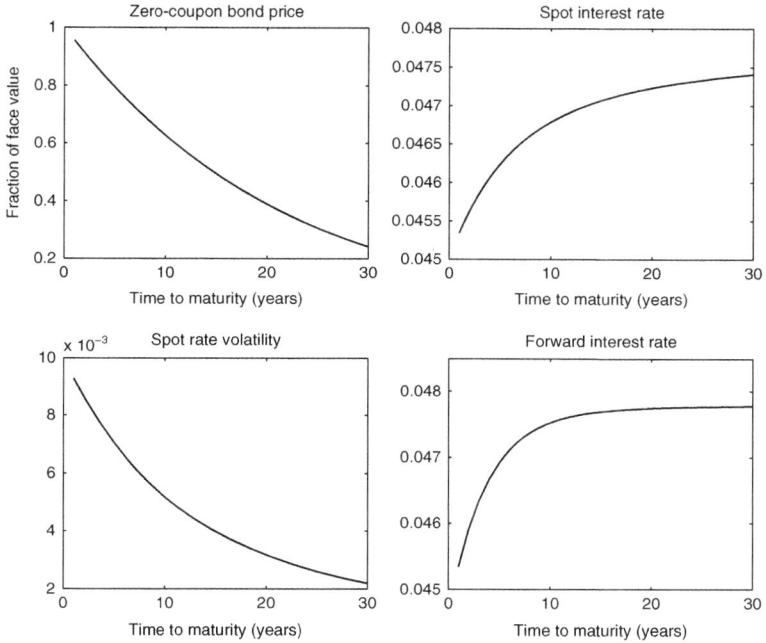

Figure 7.1 Zero-coupon bond prices, spot and forward interest rates, and spot rate volatility in the Vasicek model.

where

$$d_1 = \frac{\ln\left(\dfrac{P(t,s)}{KP(t,T)}\right)}{\sigma_p} + \frac{\sigma_p}{2},$$

$$d_2 = d_1 - \sigma_p,$$

$$\sigma_p = \frac{v(t,T)\left(1 - e^{-\kappa(s-T)}\right)}{\kappa},$$

$$v(t,T) = \sqrt{\frac{\sigma^2(1 - e^{-2\kappa(T-t)})}{2\kappa}}.$$

The Cox–Ingersoll–Ross (CIR) Model

In order to fix the somewhat embarrassing potential arbitrage possibility in the Vasicek (1977) model, Cos, Ross, and Ingersoll (1985) proposed their famous squareroot process for the short rate which has a lower bound on the short rate at zero. Unfortunately, the mathematical treatment becomes quite a bit more complicated. The starting point of the CIR model is the continuous time evolution of the short rate:

$$dr_t = \kappa(\bar{r} - r_t)dt + \sigma\sqrt{r_t}dz, \tag{7.10}$$

where all the variables are as previously defined for the Vasicek (1977) model. The present value at time t of a zero-coupon bond maturing at time $s > t$ and its associated zero-coupon yield to maturity $R(t,s)$ are given by

$$P(t,s) = A(t,s)e^{-B(t,s)r_t}, \tag{7.11}$$

$$R(t,s) = -\frac{\ln A(t,s)}{s-t} + \frac{B(t,s)}{s-t}r_t, \tag{7.12}$$

$$\sigma_R(t,s) = \frac{\sigma\sqrt{r_t}}{s-t}B(t,s), \tag{7.13}$$

where

$$A(t,s) = \left(\frac{\phi_1 e^{\phi_2(s-t)}}{\phi_2(e^{\phi_1(s-t)} - 1) + \phi_1}\right)^{\phi_3},$$

$$B(t,s) = \left(\frac{e^{\phi_1(s-t)} - 1}{\phi_2(e^{\phi_1(s-t)} - 1) + \phi_1}\right),$$

$$\phi_1 \equiv \sqrt{\kappa^2 + 2\sigma^2},$$

$$\phi_2 \equiv \frac{(\kappa + \phi_1)}{2},$$

$$\phi_3 \equiv \frac{2\kappa\bar{r}}{\sigma^2}.$$

Figure 7.2 plots the zero-coupon bond prices, spot and forward interest rates, and spot rate volatilities as a function of the time to maturity in a typical example of the CIR model with parameter values $\kappa = 0.15$, $\bar{r} = 0.05$, $r_t = 0.045$, and $\sigma = 0.01$.

A European call option on a pure discount bond has the following price:

$$c(t,T,s) = P(t,s)\chi^2\left(2r^*[\phi + \psi + B(T,s)]; \frac{4\kappa\bar{r}}{\sigma^2}, \frac{2\phi^2 re^{\theta(T-t)}}{\phi + \psi + B(T,s)}\right)$$

$$- KP(t,T)\chi^2\left(2r^*[\phi + \psi]; \frac{4\kappa\bar{r}}{\sigma^2}, \frac{2\phi^2 re^{\theta(T-t)}}{\phi + \psi}\right),$$

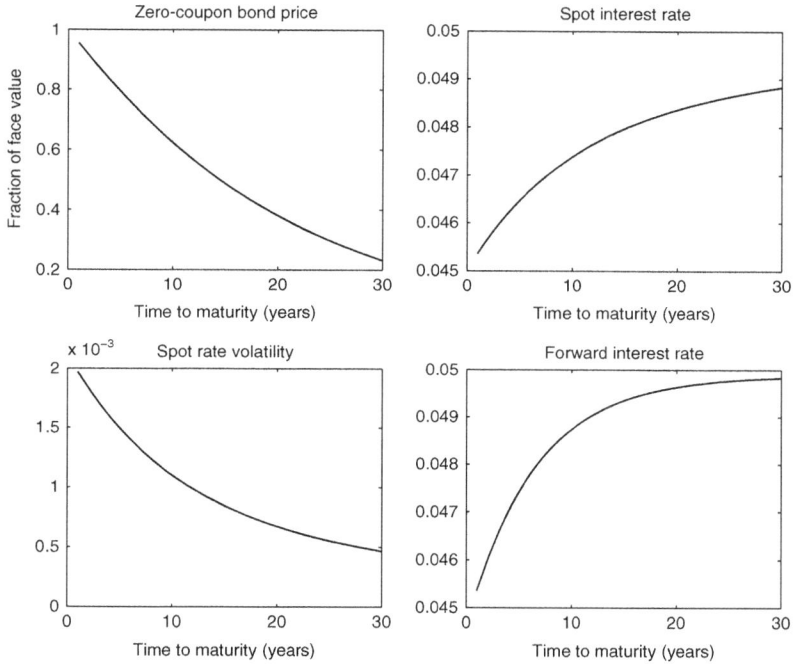

Figure 7.2 Zero-coupon bond prices, spot and forward interest rates, and spot rate volatility in the Cox–Ingersoll–Ross model.

where

$$\theta \equiv \sqrt{(\kappa^2 + 2\sigma^2)},$$

$$\phi \equiv \frac{2\theta}{\sigma^2(e^{-\theta(T-t)} - 1)},$$

$$\psi \equiv \frac{\kappa + \theta}{\sigma},$$

$$r^\star = \frac{\ln\left(\dfrac{A(T,s)}{K}\right)}{B(T,s)},$$

and $\chi^2(x; n, k)$ is the cumulative distribution function of a noncentral chi-squared random variable with a critical value of x, n degrees of freedom, and a noncentrality parameter of k.

7.1.2   Term Structure Consistent Models

Equilibrium Term Structure Volatility

Ho and Lee (1986) propose a model of the short rate as a random walk with a time-varying drift and constant volatility as follows:

$$dr = \theta(t)dt + \sigma dz, \tag{7.14}$$

where $\theta(t)$ is the time-varying drift rate of the short rate. At first glance, this appears to be a somewhat strange model for the short rate in light of empirical evidence suggesting that it is mean reverting. In other words, we do not expect the short interest rate to drift up to very large values or drift down, possibly, below zero. However, the objective of the Ho and Lee (1986) model was to give sufficient flexibility to the model so that the entire existing term structure of zero-coupon rates can be fit to the existing data.

In order to avoid any possible arbitrage opportunity, we need the following technical condition on $\theta(t)$:

$$\theta(t) = \frac{\partial f(0,t)}{\partial t} + \sigma^2 t. \tag{7.15}$$

Just as in the Vasicek (1977) model, the volatility of the zero-coupon yield is constant at all times and maturities:

$$\sigma_R(t,s) = \sigma. \tag{7.16}$$

The price at time s of a zero-coupon bond maturing at $T > s$ is once again exponentially affine:

$$P(T,s) = A(T,s)e^{-B(T,s)r(T)}, \tag{7.17}$$

where

$$B(T,s) = (s - T),$$

$$\ln A(T,s) = \ln \frac{P(t,s)}{P(t,T)} - B(T,s)\frac{\partial \ln P(t,T)}{\partial T} - \frac{1}{2}\sigma^2(T-t)B(T,s)^2,$$

and $r(T)$ denotes the level of the short rate at time T.

One popular way of discretizing the continuous time process and building a binomial tree for the short rate in the Ho and Lee (1986) model is presented in the following diagram:

Short rate

$$r_{t+2} + 2v_2$$

$$r_{t+1} + v_1$$

$$r_t$$

$$r_{t+2} + v_2$$

$$r_{t+1}$$

$$r_{t+2}$$

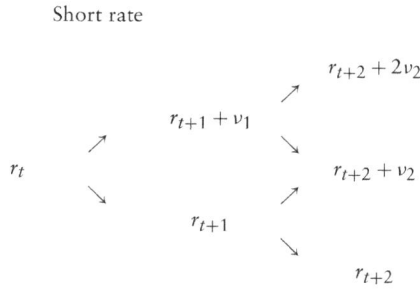

Hull and White (1990) one factor model

Hull and White (1990) propose an extension to the Vasicek (1977) and Cox, Ross, and Ingersoll (1985) interest rate models to allow the model to fit the current term structure of interest rates and either the volatilities of the zero-coupon spot interest rates or the volatilities of the forward interest rates. The model starts with the following process for the short rate:

$$dr = [\theta(t) - \alpha r]dt + \sigma dz, \tag{7.18}$$

where $\theta(t)$ is a time-varying level toward which the short rate mean reverts to and has to satisfy the following condition:

$$\theta(t) = \frac{\partial f(0,t)}{\partial t} + \alpha f(0,t) + \frac{\sigma^2}{2\alpha}(1 - e^{-2\alpha t}). \tag{7.19}$$

Hull and White (1990) show that the volatility of the spot rates varies with time to maturity in a very intuitive fashion dying out at long maturities as follows:

$$\sigma_R(t,s) = \frac{\sigma}{\alpha(s-t)}(1 - e^{-\alpha(s-t)}). \tag{7.20}$$

The price of a zero-coupon bond in this framework is exponentially affine and is given by the following:

$$P(T,s) = A(T,s)e^{-B(T,s)r(T)}, \tag{7.21}$$

where

$$B(T,s) = \frac{1}{\alpha}(1 - e^{-\alpha(s-T)}),$$

$$A(T,s) = \ln\frac{P(t,s)}{P(t,T)} - B(T,s)\frac{\partial \ln P(t,T)}{\partial T}$$

$$-\frac{1}{4\alpha^3}(e^{-\alpha(s-t)} - e^{-\alpha(T-t)})^2(e^{2\alpha(T-t)} - 1).$$

The prices of European options on zero-coupon discount bonds within the Hull and White (1990) model are given by

$$c(t,T,s) = P(t,s)N(d_1) - KP(t,T)N(d_2), \tag{7.22}$$

$$p(t,T,s) = KP(t,T)N(-d_2) - P(t,s)N(-d_1), \tag{7.23}$$

where

$$d_1 = \frac{\ln(P(t,s)/KP(t,T))}{\sigma_P} + \frac{\sigma_P}{2},$$

$$d_2 = d_1 - \sigma_P,$$

$$\sigma_P^2 = \frac{\sigma^2}{2\alpha^3}(1 - e^{-2\alpha(T-t)})(1 - e^{-\alpha(s-T)})^2.$$

Black, Derman, and Toy (1990) propose an additive model for the short rate best illustrated in the following diagram:

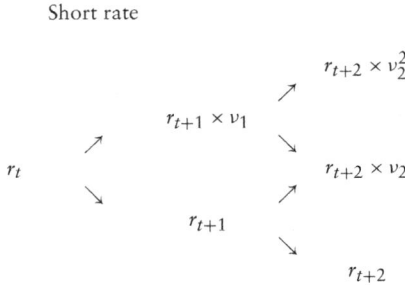

Short rate

$$r_{t+2} \times v_2^2$$

$$r_{t+1} \times v_1$$

$$r_t$$

$$r_{t+2} \times v_2$$

$$r_{t+1}$$

$$r_{t+2}$$

The continuous time version of the short rate is given by the following equation:

$$d\ln r(t) = \left[\theta(t) + \frac{\sigma'(t)}{\sigma(t)}\ln r(t)\right]dt + \sigma(t)dz, \tag{7.24}$$

which allows for, possibly, time-varying volatility of the zero-coupon yield volatility.

A popular version of this model with practitioners keeps the future short-rate volatility constant in which case the stochastic process for the short rate is simplified to the following:

$$d\ln r = \theta(t)dt + \sigma dz, \tag{7.25}$$

which is also known as the log-normal version of the Ho–Lee model.

Black and Karasinski (1991) propose an even more flexible model with the following stochastic process for the short rate:

$$d\ln r = [\theta(t) - \alpha(t)\ln r] + \sigma(t)dz, \tag{7.26}$$

which has the advantage of always having a strictly positive short rate. The discretized version of this model has the added flexibility of time varying lengths of the time steps between successive nodes in the binomial tree for the short rate. This allows us to better fit the existing empirical data about the term structure of yields and their volatilities. A simplified version of this model with a time invariant $\alpha(t)$ has the following stochastic evolution of the short rate:

$$d\ln r = [\theta(t) - \alpha\ln r]dt + \sigma dz. \tag{7.27}$$

Fit Term Structure Volatility

Heath, Jarrow, and Morton (1990, 1992) propose one of the most general model of the term structure of interest rates and their volatilities by allowing the entire sequence of forward rates to move stochastically over time. The best way to depict their model is by the following simple diagram:

Forward rate

$$r_{t+2} = f(t+2, t+2)$$

$$r_{t+1} = f(t+1, t+1)$$
$$f(t+1, t+2)$$

$$r_t = f(t,t)$$
$$f(t, t+1)$$
$$f(t, t+2)$$

$$r_{t+2} = f(t+2, t+2)$$

$$r_{t+1} = f(t+1, t+1)$$
$$f(t+1, t+2)$$

$$r_{t+2} = f(t+2, t+2)$$

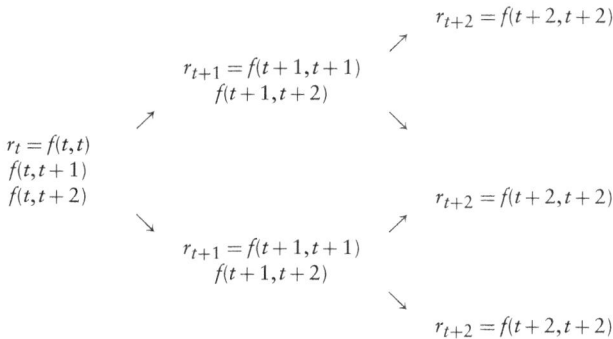

Note that this modeling approach allows us to model changes in the level, slope, and curvature of the entire term structure of interest rates. We can comfortably fit the term structure of zero-coupon yields and their volatilities or the volatilities of the forward interest rates. The binomial version will essentially be a one-factor model but more factors are possible. For example, a trinomial tree will have two distinct factors driving the evolution of the term structure of interest rates.

7.2   Binomial Term Structure Models

7.2.1   Pricing a Fixed-Coupon Risk-Free Bond

The following diagram illustrates the pricing of a fixed-coupon risk-free bond. For simplicity, we have not built any mean reversion in the short rate and have left the risk-neutral probabilities at 50% at each node of the binomial tree.

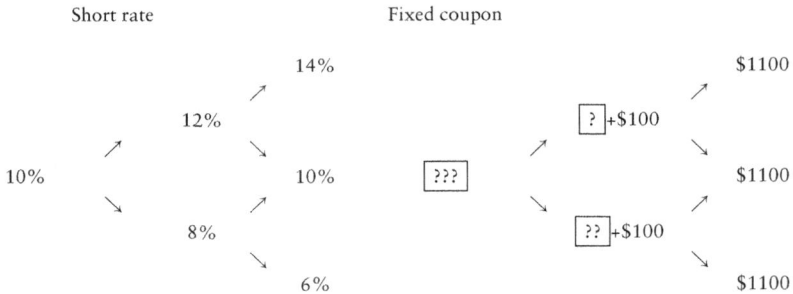

Short rate   Fixed coupon


```
Short rate                                    Fixed coupon

                        14%                                              $1100
                    ↗                                              ↗
            12%                                       ? +$100
        ↗            ↘                            ↗            ↘
10%                      10%          ???                            $1100
        ↘            ↗                            ↘            ↗
            8%                                        ?? +$100
                    ↘                                              ↘
                        6%                                               $1100
```

Suppose for the sake of simplicity that in our short rate model all risk-neutral probabilities in all nodes of the tree are equal to 50% (so that there is no mean reversion and the short rate follows a random walk). Therefore, we can fill in the unknown quantities about the intermediate values of the FRN as well as its ex-coupon value at time $t = 0$:

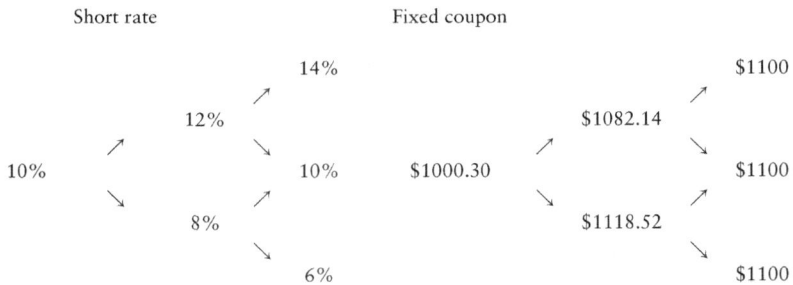

```
Short rate                                    Fixed coupon

                        14%                                              $1100
                    ↗                                              ↗
            12%                                       $1082.14
        ↗            ↘                            ↗            ↘
10%                      10%          $1000.30                       $1100
        ↘            ↗                            ↘            ↗
            8%                                        $1118.52
                    ↘                                              ↘
                        6%                                               $1100
```

where

$$\$1082.14 = \frac{0.5 \times \$1100 + 0.5 \times \$1100}{1.2} + \$100,$$

$$\$1118.52 = \frac{0.5 \times \$1100 + 0.5 \times \$1100}{1.08} + \$100,$$

$$\$1000.30 = \frac{0.5 \times \$1082.14 + 0.5 \times \$1118.52}{1.1}.$$

7.2.2   Pricing a Risk-Free FRN

The next security to consider pricing is the plain vanilla FRN. The following diagram illustrates the binomial tree for the short rate and the pricing of the FRN at every node of the tree:

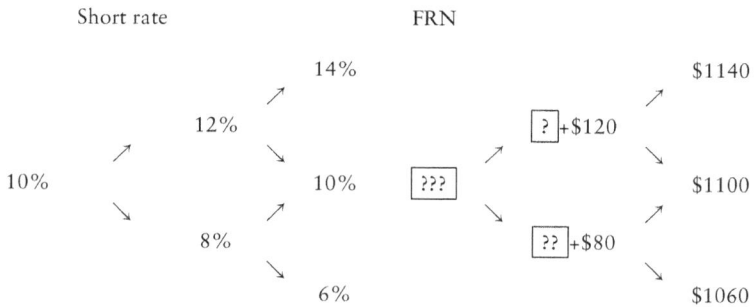

Short rate   FRN

		14%		$1140
	12% ↗		? +$120 ↗	
10% ↗	↘	10%	↗ ??? ↘	$1100 ↗
↘	8% ↗	↗	?? +$80 ↗	
	↘	6%	↘	$1060

Suppose for the sake of simplicity that in our short rate model all risk-neutral probabilities in all nodes of the tree are equal to 50% (so that there is no mean reversion and the short rate follows a random walk). Therefore, we can fill in the unknown quantities about the intermediate values of the FRN as well as its ex-coupon value at time $t = 0$:

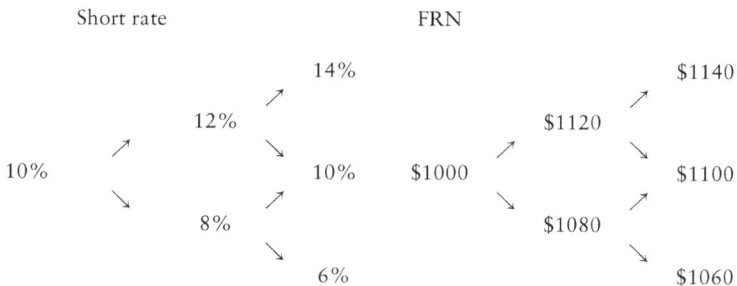

Short rate   FRN

		14%		$1140
	12% ↗		$1120 ↗	
10% ↗	↘	10%	$1000 ↗ ↘	$1100 ↗
↘	8% ↗	↗	$1080 ↗	
	↘	6%	↘	$1060

where

$$\$1120 = \frac{0.5 \times \$1140 + 0.5 \times \$1100}{1.2} + \$120,$$

$$\$1080 = \frac{0.5 \times \$1100 + 0.5 \times \$1060}{1.08} + \$80,$$

$$\$1000 = \frac{0.5 \times \$1120 + 0.5 \times \$1080}{1.1}.$$

7.2.3 An Interest Rate Swap

Now we are ready to consider pricing the fixed leg of an interest rate swap given a floating leg that pays the short rate. All we need to do is find a fixed coupon for a fixed-coupon bond that will have the same price as the FRN. In the example above, it turns out that the fixed coupon should be 9.9827% and the fixed-coupon bond has a present value of $1000 which is the same as the FRN. Therefore, we will say that the swap rate is 9.9827% in exchange for receiving the short rate.

7.2.4 Adjustable-Rate Mortgages

Conceptually, an adjustable-rate mortgages (ARM) is very similar to an FRN. However, where things get interesting is when we consider all the embedded options that are bundled with an ARM in practice. These typically include "lifetime" limits on the interest rate (over the life of the mortgage) and annual limits on the increase/decrease of the interest rate.

7.2.5 Pricing an Interest Rate Cap/Caption

Next, let us consider an interest rate cap which is very similar to a continuous call option on the short rate. It pays off the difference between the short rate and the capped rate, if positive, and zero otherwise on a notional value, in every period until the maturity of the cap. The following diagram illustrates the pricing of a cap with two periods to maturity with a capped rate of 7% on a $1000 notional value:

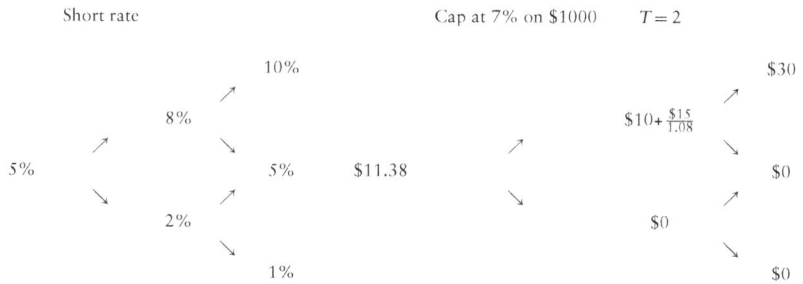

Short rate   Cap at 7% on $1000 $T = 2$

```
                  10%                                              $30
               ↗                                              ↗
         8%                                    $10+$\frac{$15}{1.08}$
      ↗       ↘                             ↗              ↘
5%            5%     $11.38                                      $0
      ↘       ↗                             ↘              ↗
         2%                                    $0
               ↘                                              ↗
                  1%                                              $0
                                                              ↘
                                                                 $0
```

A related interest rate derivative to consider is the caption or a call option on a cap. The reason captions exist is that caps tend to be expensive especially those with long maturities. If we are not certain, we want to enter a cap right away: we may instead purchase a caption which gives us the option to acquire a cap for a fixed price. The following diagram illustrates a caption with a strike price of $12 and one period to maturity:

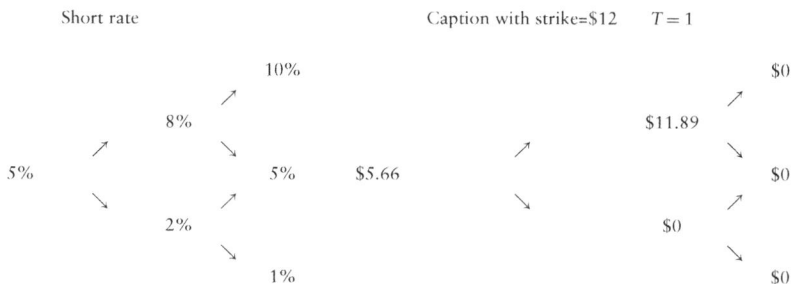

Short rate   Caption with strike=$12 $T = 1$

```
                  10%                                              $0
               ↗                                              ↗
         8%                                    $11.89
      ↗       ↘                             ↗              ↘
5%            5%     $5.66                                      $0
      ↘       ↗                             ↘              ↗
         2%                                    $0
               ↘                                              ↗
                  1%                                              $0
                                                              ↘
                                                                 $0
```

7.2.6   Pricing an Interest Rate Floor/Flotion

For the purposes of interest rate risk hedging, a bond investor might consider acquiring an interest rate floor which is very similar to a put option on the value of the short interest rate. In every period before the floor's maturity, it pays off the difference between the floor rate and the short rate, if positive, and zero otherwise. The following diagram illustrates the valuation of a floor with a floor rate of 2% on a $1000 notional value:

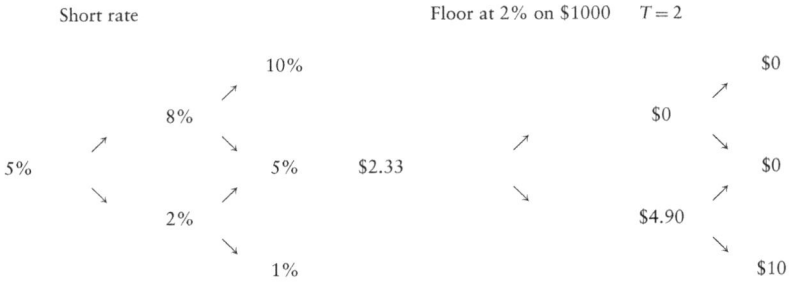

Short rate   Floor at 2% on $1000 $T = 2$

```
                    10%                                                          $0
              8%                                                    $0
        5%              5%      $2.33                                      $0
              2%                                                    $4.90
                    1%                                                          $10
```

Note that the floor is in the money only at the bottom states of the world in the middle and the last time period. An option to enter a floor for a fixed price at a future point in time is also available and is referred to as a flotion. The next diagram prices a flotion to enter the above floor for a strike price of $4 and mature in the middle time period:

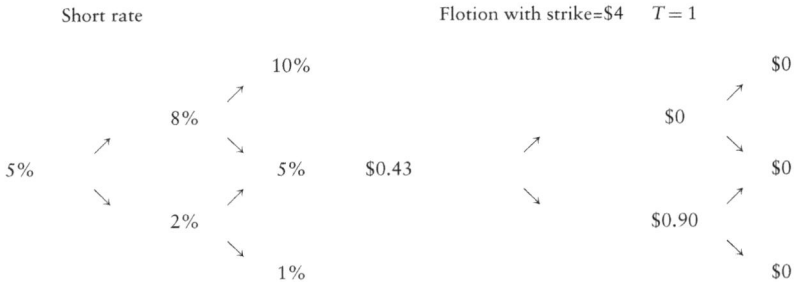

Short rate   Flotion with strike=$4 $T = 1$

```
                    10%                                                          $0
              8%                                                    $0
        5%              5%      $0.43                                      $0
              2%                                                    $0.90
                    1%                                                          $0
```

Note, once again, that the flotion is much cheaper than the floor.

Various combinations of the cap and floor generate a wide variety of payoff contingent on the future values of the short rate. For example, a 2/7 collar consists of a long position in a 7% cap and a short position in 2% floor. Note that the price of this collar is $11.38 − $2.33 = $9.05. It is clearly cheaper to acquire than to buy the cap. Unfortunately, it also puts a lower limit on the interest rate that is to be paid, namely, 2%.

7.2.7   Pricing a Reverse Floater

As out final example of exotic interest rate instruments, let us consider how we would price an inverse floater with an annual coupon rate of $30\% - 2 \times r$, where r is the short rate. The following diagram illustrates the pricing of this inverse floater:

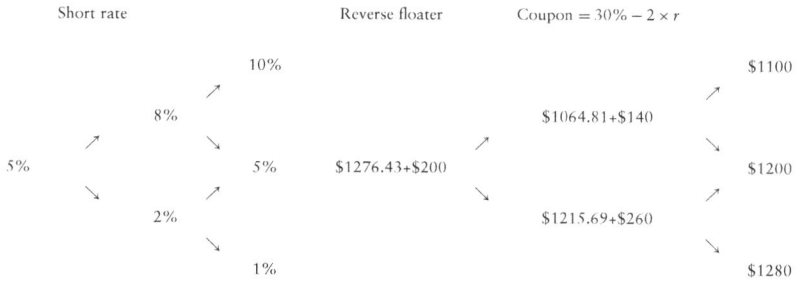

Short rate	Reverse floater	Coupon = $30\% - 2 \times r$

```
Short rate                  Reverse floater        Coupon = 30% − 2 × r

                    10%                                             $1100
                 ↗                                               ↗
            8%                                  $1064.81+$140
         ↗      ↘                                           ↘
   5%             5%      $1276.43+$200              ↗              $1200
         ↘      ↗                                           ↗
            2%                                  $1215.69+$260
                 ↘                                               ↘
                    1%                                              $1280
```

Note how this security loses value quickly as the short rate increases and gains in value substantially as the short rate declines. This is indeed the purpose for which the inverse floater was created.

Problems

1. Prove that in the simple version of the Ho–Lee model all zero-coupon spot and forward interest rates are nonnegative as long as the short rates at every node in the binomial tree are nonnegative and all risk-neutral probabilities are proper probabilities.
2. Consider a binomial model for the short rate starting at 5% at $t=0$ and going up or down by 1% in each period over the next two periods with a 50% risk-neutral probability at each node. Find the present value of an exotic security payoff the short rate at every node of the tree. How would we replicate this exotic security using zero-coupon bonds of various maturities? In other words, what is the dynamic replicating portfolio for the short rate?
3. Consider the binomial models for the pricing of the interest rate cap and the interest rate floor earlier in this chapter. Design an interest rate collar consisting of a long position in the interest rate cap and a short position in the interest rate floor such that the net cost of entering the interest rate corridor at inception is zero, i.e., the cap and the floor must have equal value.

8

Foreign Exchange

8.1   Spot and Forward Commodity Prices

8.1.1   Purchasing Power Parity

Let i_h be the periodic inflation rate in the home country, i_f be the periodic inflation rate in the foreign country, e_0 be the spot exchange rate given by the current home currency value of 1 unit of foreign currency, and e_t be the period t home currency value of 1 unit of foreign currency.

The absolute version of the purchasing power parity (PPP) states that in an idealized world with no taxes, tariffs, transaction or transportation costs, identical goods should sell for the same price everywhere, provided markets for goods are perfectly competitive and capital markets are integrated:

$$\frac{e_t}{e_0} = \left(\frac{1+i_h}{1+i_f} \right)^t . \tag{8.1}$$

A special case of this is obtained when we consider $t = 1$ and the one-period change in the exchange rate:

$$\frac{e_1}{e_0} = \frac{1+i_h}{1+i_f}, \tag{8.2}$$

or, more intuitively expressed as

$$\frac{e_1 - e_0}{e_0} = \frac{i_h - i_f}{1+i_f}. \tag{8.3}$$

Note that this means that in an ideal world the expected percentage change in the exchange rate will be, approximately, driven by the inflation differential between the home and foreign country.

Example: Suppose the current US price level is at 112 and the Swiss price level is at 107 relative to a base price level of 100 for both countries. If the initial value of the Swiss frank was $0.58, then according to PPP, the dollar value of the Swiss frank should have risen to $0.58 \times (112/107) = 0.6071 or an appreciation of 4.67%.

Alternatively, if the current Swiss price level equals 119 instead, then according to PPP, the current dollar value of the Swiss frank should have fallen to $0.58 \times (112/119) = 0.5459 or a depreciation of 5.88%.

In practice, we can imagine many if not all of the assumptions behind the derivation of PPP will fail to obtain. Consequently, the empirical evidence on PPP is mixed, at least at short time horizons. Once good markets and capital markets have had some time to adjust, then PPP tends to hold roughly in relative terms in the long run. Nevertheless, significant deviation is obtained in the short run which are mostly due to taxes, tariffs, and various other market imperfections. More importantly, the basket of goods used to calculate inflation rates may differ from country to country due to heterogeneous local tastes. Furthermore, many services are not easy or even impossible to trade across borders.[1]

8.2   Spot and Forward Exchange Rates

Let us first consider the case of two currencies and a single spot exchange rate. For simplicity, let us express the exchange rate as units of home currency per unit of foreign currency. Expressing the exchange rate in opposite terms leads to an interesting nonlinearity. For example, consider a spot exchange rate of 100¥/$ which moves to 80¥/$. This change in the exchange rate represents a 20% depreciation of the dollar versus the yen. At the same time, from the point of view of the yen as home currency this change represents a move from 0.01$/¥ to 0.0125$/¥ which is a 25% appreciation of the yen versus the dollar. This mathematical curiosity is sometimes referred to as Seigel's paradox. It disappears completely if we use percentage log changes in exchange rates rather than simple percentage changes in exchange rates.

Next, let us introduce a buy and a sell spot exchange rate or, more formally, an ask and a bid exchange rate, respectively, $e_{h/f}^{ASK}$ and

$e_{b/f}^{BID}$. The first interesting question to address is how do these two rates link with the respective ask and bid rates when the exchange rate is expressed in opposite terms. Insisting that there is no free lunch in trading, these two currencies leads to the following:

$$e_{b/f}^{ASK} \leq \frac{1}{e_{f/b}^{BID}}, \tag{8.4}$$

$$e_{b/f}^{BID} \leq \frac{1}{e_{f/b}^{ASK}}. \tag{8.5}$$

The proof of the above is quite simple and is left as an exercise for the reader. The intuition behind this result is quite straightforward. It simply has to do with the fact that the act of purchasing foreign currency with home currency is equivalent to selling home currency in exchange of foreign currency.

8.2.1   Triangular Arbitrage with Bid-Ask Spread

First, start with 1 unit of currency X, exchange it for currency Y, then exchange currency Y for currency Z. Finally, sell currency Z for currency X. In order to avoid arbitrage, we should end up with at most 1 unit of currency X at the end or less. This leads to the following restriction on the ask exchange rates:

$$e_{Y/X}^{ASK} \times e_{Z/Y}^{ASK} \times e_{X/Y}^{ASK} \geq 1. \tag{8.6}$$

To derive a similar constraint on the bid exchange rates, let us try trading in the opposite direction. Suppose we start with 1 unit of currency Z, exchange it for currency X, which we then exchange into currency Y. Finally, we revert to the original currency we started with. These trades should leave with no more than 1 unit of currency Z or less. We can express this more formally as:

$$e_{X/Z}^{BID} \times e_{Y/X}^{BID} \times e_{Z/Y}^{BID} \leq 1. \tag{8.7}$$

8.2.2   Interest Rate Parity

Before we formally derive the interest rate parity relationships, let us consider the following two strategies involving two currencies with spot and forward exchange rates. For simplicity, we will first consider an idealized world where we can buy and sell at the same price both spot and forward.

Starting with borrowing 1 unit of home currency at time $t = 0$ at the home currency interest rate r_h, we exchange it at the spot exchange rate for $1/e_0$ units of foreign currency. We lend the $1/e_0$ units of foreign currency at the foreign interest rate of r_f for one period. This leaves us with $(1 + r_f)/e_0$ units of foreign currency at $t = 1$. Simultaneously, at time $t = 0$ we enter a forward exchange contract to sell $(1 + r_f)/e_0$ units of foreign currency for home currency at the forward exchange rate f_1. This leaves us with $(1 + r_f)f_1/e_0$ units of home currency at $t = 1$ with which we can repay our loan coming due at $t = 1$ in the amount of $(1 + r_h)$. In order to avoid arbitrage, we should be allowed to make a risk-free profit but we can at best break even or suffer a loss.

A second alternative strategy involves borrowing 1 unit of foreign currency at $t = 0$ at the foreign interest rate r_f which we exchange at the spot exchange rate for home currency at the rate of e_0 leaving us with e_0 units of home currency at $t = 0$. We lend these e_0 units of home currency at the home interest rate r_h which brings us $e_0(1 + r_h)$ units of home currency at $t = 1$. At the same time, we enter a forward exchange contract to sell $e_0(1 + r_h)$ units of home currency for foreign currency leaving us with $e_0(1 + r_h)/f_1$ units of foreign currency at $t = 1$. Our foreign currency loan is coming due at $t = 1$ as well and we need to pay back $(1 + r_f)$ units of foreign currency. Once again, in order to avoid arbitrage, we should have accumulated barely enough money in order to be able to pay back our debt and should not be making a risk-free profit.

Mathematically, the above two statements can conveniently be expressed with the following inequalities:

$$\frac{f_1(1 + r_f)}{e_0} - (1 + r_h) \leq 0, \tag{8.8}$$

$$\frac{e_0(1 + r_h)}{f_1} - (1 + r_f) \leq 0. \tag{8.9}$$

Simplifying the above two we obtain:

$$\frac{f_1(1 + r_f)}{e_0(1 + r_h)} \leq 1, \tag{8.10}$$

$$\frac{e_0(1 + r_h)}{f_1(1 + r_f)} \leq 1. \tag{8.11}$$

Both of the above inequalities can be true if and only if interest rate parity holds:

$$\frac{f_1}{e_0} = \frac{1 + r_b}{1 + r_f}. \tag{8.12}$$

The above expression is usually referred to as interest rate parity. Note that this is a hard constraint, i.e., even a small deviation from it can lead to arbitrage profits assuming that we can freely buy and sell both currencies spot at e_0 and forward at f_1 as well as freely borrow and lend currency units at home and abroad at r_b and r_f, respectively. Let us trace out the implications of this claim. If $(1 + r_b) < (1 + r_f)\frac{f_1}{e_0}$, then it is cheaper to borrow at home, acquire foreign currency, and lend abroad at no risk to one's own funds. Moreover, if this inequality persists for a while in the absence of any capital or banking controls then eventually funds will flow from the home country into the foreign country pushing down the forward exchange rate bringing it back into equilibrium. Similarly, if $(1 + r_b) > (1 + r_f)\frac{f_1}{e_0}$ then it is cheaper to borrow abroad, exchange the foreign currency for home currency, and lend it at home. Once again, if this situation persists for a while then foreign funds will flow into the home country and increase the forward exchange rate back to equality.

The above is also occasionally referred to as covered interest rate parity where the cover refers to the use of a forward exchange contract. The uncovered version of interest rate parity is risky and is commonly referred to as the carry trade. To illustrate the uncovered interest parity relation, we will have to repeat the two steps above but instead of buying and selling currency at the forward exchange rate we will trade at the future spot exchange rate. The latter is uncertain from the points of view of $t = 0$ and we will denote it as $\tilde{e}_1$. Note that the only way we can profit by trading only in the spot exchange rate markets is if the following two inequalities hold true at the actual value of the exchange rate next period, e_1:

$$\frac{e_1(1 + r_f)}{e_0(1 + r_b)} \leq 1, \tag{8.13}$$

$$\frac{e_0(1 + r_b)}{e_1(1 + r_f)} \leq 1. \tag{8.14}$$

However, it is quite possible that either or both of these inequalities are violated by the time we enter time period $t = 1$ in which case the carry trade will suffer a loss.

It is easy to generalize the covered interest rate parity relation to the case where we have realistic bid and ask exchange rates as well as differential interest rates for borrowing and lending. First, let us consider the simplest complication of a bid–ask spread in the spot foreign exchange market. Let us denote the spot bid exchange rate (this is the rate at which we sell foreign currency for home currency) by e_0^{BID} and the spot ask exchange rate (this is the rate at which we buy foreign currency with home currency) by e_0^{ASK}. Due to the "wedge" driven by the bid–ask spread in the spot exchange rate, there will be a corresponding "wedge" or bid–ask spread in the forward rate. Let us denote the forward bid exchange rate (this is the rate at which we sell foreign currency forward for home currency) by f_1^{BID} and the forward ask exchange rate (this is the rate at which we buy forward foreign currency with home currency) by f_1^{ASK}.

Returning again to our two arbitrage strategies, we require that they both yield nonpositive returns which can be mathematically expressed as follows:

$$\frac{f_1^{\text{BID}}}{e_0^{\text{ASK}}(1+r_f)} - (1+r_h) \leq 0, \tag{8.15}$$

$$\frac{e_0^{\text{BID}}(1+r_h)}{f_1^{\text{ASK}}} - (1+r_f) \leq 0. \tag{8.16}$$

These two inequalities can be simplified to

$$\frac{f_1^{\text{BID}}}{e_0^{\text{ASK}}} \leq \frac{(1+r_h)}{(1+r_f)}, \tag{8.17}$$

$$\frac{f_1^{\text{ASK}}}{e_0^{\text{BID}}} \geq \frac{(1+r_h)}{(1+r_f)}. \tag{8.18}$$

Finally, in addition to the bid–ask spread, we are going to introduce another complication, namely, differential rates for borrowing and lending. Let us denote the home country's borrowing and lending interest rates by r_h^B and r_h^L. Similarly, r_f^B and r_f^L will be the foreign country's borrowing and lending interest rates, respectively.

Going back to our two arbitrage strategies, we again require that they generate no positive profit which summarizes to the following:

$$\frac{f_1^{BID}(1+r_f^L)}{e_0^{ASK}} - (1+r_b^B) \leq 0, \tag{8.19}$$

$$\frac{e_0^{BID}(1+r_b^L)}{f_1^{ASK}} - (1+r_f^B) \leq 0. \tag{8.20}$$

The latter can be rearranged as follows:

$$\frac{f_1^{BID}}{e_0^{ASK}} \leq \frac{(1+r_b^B)}{(1+r_f^L)}, \tag{8.21}$$

$$\frac{f_1^{ASK}}{e_0^{BID}} \geq \frac{(1+r_b^L)}{(1+r_f^B)}. \tag{8.22}$$

8.3   Foreign Exchange Capital Budgeting

Before we delve into the general case of discounting foreign exchange rate denominated cash flows, let us consider a somewhat simplified example. A Turkish multinational corporation has the following cash flows in home currency, YTL, and foreign currency, USD, over the next 3 years:

Currency	$t=1$	$t=2$	$t=3$
YTL	10	15	20
USD	5	6	7

The following risk-free rates prevail on both countries:

Currency	r_1	r_2	r_3
YTL	15%	14%	12%
USD	4%	5%	6%

The company's beta with respect to the world portfolio is 1.2. The world portfolio has constant expected returns over the next 3 years of 16% in YTL terms. Finally, the spot exchange rate is 1.36 YTL/USD.

We already established what the USD expected returns on the world market portfolio are and what the USD discount rates are over the next 3 years:

	$t = 1$	$t = 2$	$t = 3$
$\bar{r}_{w,\$}$	4.91%	6.84%	9.78%
$\bar{r}_{w,\text{YTL}}$	16%	16%	16%
$f_{\text{YTL}/\$}$	1.5038	1.6031	1.6043
$d_{\text{MNC},\$}$	5.09%	7.21%	10.54%
$d_{\text{MNC},\text{YTL}}$	16.2%	16.4%	16.8%

Let us first consider the case of a completely segmented world model. Locally, CAPM holds in every country. Recall our international investments formulae:

$$w_h = \frac{\bar{r}_{m,h} - r_h}{\gamma_h \sigma_h^2}, \tag{8.23}$$

$$w_f = \frac{\bar{r}_{m,f} - r_f}{\gamma_f \sigma_f^2}. \tag{8.24}$$

In equilibrium, both investors have to hold their entire stock markets which implies that their stock markets risk premia are

$$\bar{r}_{m,h} = r_h + \gamma_h \sigma_h^2, \tag{8.25}$$

$$\bar{r}_{f,h} = r_f + \gamma_f \sigma_f^2. \tag{8.26}$$

Any specific home/foreign company will have the following expected returns:

$$\bar{r}_{i,h} = r_h + \beta_{i,h} \bar{r}_{m,h}, \tag{8.27}$$

$$\bar{r}_{i,f} = r_f + \beta_{i,f} \bar{r}_{m,f}. \tag{8.28}$$

Both companies expected returns are in local currency terms. Next, let us consider the case of a perfectly integrated world model. In order to proceed we need to make some assumptions. First, we will assume that capital markets are completely integrated; there are no trade barriers and no transaction costs. Second, we will assume that the international CAPM holds. This implies that all securities excess expected returns are proportional to the excess return on the world portfolio as follows:

$$\bar{r}_{i,h} = r_h + \beta_{i,h}\bar{r}_{w,h}, \tag{8.29}$$

$$\bar{r}_{i,f} = r_f + \beta_{i,f}\bar{r}_{w,f}. \tag{8.30}$$

Convert all foreign currency cash flows to home currency using forward exchange rates. Finally, obtain the present value using home currency discount rates. Next, we need an estimate of the world market risk premium and compute multicurrency discount rates to obtain the foreign currency present values. Finally, we convert all foreign currency present values back to home currency using spot exchange rates.

Let us present these ideas using a simplified example. A Turkish multinational company has the following YTL and USD cash flows over the next 3 years:

Currency	$t=1$	$t=2$	$t=3$
YTL	10	15	20
USD	5	6	7

The following zero-coupon risk-free rates prevail in both countries:

Currency	r_1	r_2	r_3
YTL	15%	14%	12%
USD	4%	5%	6%

The company's beta with respect to the world portfolio is 1.2. The world portfolio has constant expected returns over the next 3 years of 16% in YTL terms. Finally, the spot exchange rate is 1.36 YTL/USD. What is the YTL/USD present value of the company's cash flows?

It is easier to do the YTL cash flows first, so let us do that:

$$PV_{YTL,CF} = \frac{10}{1 + 0.15 + 1.2 \cdot (0.16 - 0.15)}$$

$$+ \frac{15}{(1 + 0.14 + 1.2 \cdot (0.16 - 0.14))^2}$$

$$+ \frac{20}{(1 + 0.12 + 1.2 \cdot (0.16 - 0.12))^3}$$

$$= \frac{10}{1.162} + \frac{15}{(1.164)^2} + \frac{20}{(1.168)^3}$$
$$= 8.61 + 11.07 + 12.55$$
$$= 32.23.$$

Now let us move on to the USD cash flows. There are three (equivalent) ways to obtain their present value. First, let us compute the implied forward exchange rates and convert the USD cash flows to YTL, then reuse the YTL discount rates:

$$f_1 = 1.36 \times \frac{1.15}{1.04} = 1.5038 \text{ YTL/USD},$$

$$f_2 = 1.36 \times \frac{(1.14)^2}{(1.05)^2} = 1.6031 \text{ YTL/USD},$$

$$f_3 = 1.36 \times \frac{(1.12)^3}{(1.06)^3} = 1.6043 \text{ YTL/USD},$$

$$PV_{USD,CF} = \frac{5 \times 1.5038}{1.162} + \frac{6 \times 1.6031}{(1.164)^2} + \frac{7 \times 1.6043}{(1.168)^3}$$
$$= \frac{7.519}{1.162} + \frac{9.6186}{(1.164)^2} + \frac{11.2301}{(1.168)^3}$$
$$= 6.47 + 7.10 + 7.05$$
$$= 20.62.$$

The second approach we take is to compute the USD discount rates and convert the USD cash flows to obtain the USD net present value, then convert to YTL at the spot exchange rate. In order to obtain the USD discount rates, we can adjust the YTL discount rates for the respective annualized forward exchange discount/premium as follows:

$$1 + d_{USD,1} = (1 + d_{YTL,1}) \times \left(\frac{e_0}{f_1} \right)$$

$$= (1.162) \times \left(\frac{1.36}{1.5038} \right) = 1.05088$$

$$\Rightarrow d_{USD,1} \approx 5.09\%,$$

$$1 + d_{USD,2} = (1 + d_{YTL,2}) \times \left(\frac{e_0}{f_2} \right)^{1/2}$$

$$= (1.164) \times \left(\frac{1.36}{1.6031} \right)^{1/2} = 1.07212$$

$$\Rightarrow d_{\text{USD},2} \approx 7.21\%,$$

$$1 + d_{\text{USD},3} = (1 + d_{\text{YTL},3}) \times \left(\frac{e_0}{f_3} \right)^{1/3}$$

$$= (1.168) \times \left(\frac{1.36}{1.6043} \right)^{1/3} = 1.10542$$

$$\Rightarrow d_{\text{USD},3} \approx 10.54\%,$$

$$\text{PV}_{\text{USD},\text{CF}} = 1.36 \times \left(\frac{5}{1.0509} + \frac{6}{(1.0721)^2} + \frac{7}{(1.1054)^3} \right)$$

$$= 1.36 \times (4.76 + 5.22 + 5.18)$$

$$= 1.36 \times 15.16$$

$$= 20.62.$$

The third way to solve this capital budgeting problem involves finding out the USD expected return on the world portfolio, converting all cash flows to USD and discounting at the dollar discount rates we found in the second approach above. Using interest rate parity, we can show that

$$\bar{r}^{\$}_{w,1} = 0.04908,$$

$$\bar{r}^{\$}_{w,2} = 0.06843,$$

$$\bar{r}^{\$}_{w,3} = 0.09785,$$

$$d_{\text{USD},1} = 0.04 + 1.2 \times (0.04908 - 0.04) \approx 5.09\%,$$

$$d_{\text{USD},2} = 0.05 + 1.2 \times (0.06843 - 0.05) \approx 7.21\%,$$

$$d_{\text{USD},3} = 0.06 + 1.2 \times (0.09785 - 0.06) \approx 10.54\%.$$

8.4   Currency Option Valuation

Plain vanilla currency options exist allowing us to prespecify the exchange rate at which we can purchase or sell foreign currency at a future point in time. A more interesting example of a foreign currency option from a valuation point of view is an option delivering a payoff in foreign currency, i.e., a digital option paying either 1 unit of foreign currency when it appreciates and zero units of foreign currency when it depreciates. Consider the following digital foreign currency option paying off £1 or £0 contingent on the USD/£exchange rate:

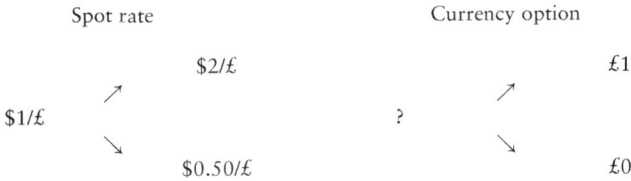

Spot rate	Currency option
$2/£	£1
$1/£ ?	
$0.50/£	£0

The best way to approach the valuation of this digital foreign currency option is to set up a replicating portfolio involving the foreign and home currency risk-free bonds for which we will need to specify a binomial tree as follows:

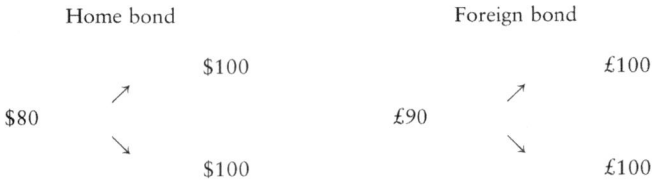

Home bond	Foreign bond
$100	£100
$80	£90
$100	£100

In order to value the USD/£ digital option, we construct a replicating portfolio of foreign currency bought at the spot market and borrowing/lending in the home risk-free asset. Let us denote the number of foreign currency units purchased spot with N_s and the number of home currency risk-free bonds purchased with N_b. Also, let the spot exchange rate be denoted as e_0 with next period values e_1^u and e_1^d, respectively, for the up and down movement in the binomial tree. Next, let today's home risk-free bond price be B_0. And, finally, let the currency option have payoffs more denoted generically as C_1^u and C_1^d, respectively, in the up and down state of the world at date $t = 1$.

We need to have the replicating portfolio fulfill the following constraints:

$$C_1^u \times e_1^u = N_s \times e_1^u(1 + r_f) + N_b \times B_0(1 + r_b), \tag{8.31}$$

$$C_1^d \times e_1^d = N_s \times e_1^d(1 + r_f) + N_b \times B_0(1 + r_b). \tag{8.32}$$

Solving the above system yields the following:

$$N_s = \frac{C_1^u e_1^u - C_1^d e_1^d}{(e_1^u - e_1^d)(1 + r_f)},$$ (8.33)

$$N_b = \frac{C_1^u\left(\dfrac{-e_1^u e_1^d}{e_1^u - e_1^d}\right) + C_1^d\left(\dfrac{e_1^d e_1^u}{e_1^u - e_1^d}\right)}{B_0(1 + r_b)}.$$ (8.34)

Now we are ready to figure out the value of the currency option at time $t = 0$, C_0. It will simply be equal to the value of the replicating portfolio of spot currency and home country risk-free bond today at $t = 0$ or, specifically:

$$C_0 = N_s \times e_0 + N_b \times B_0,$$ (8.35)

$$= \left(\frac{1}{1 + r_b}\right)\left\{C_1^u e_1^u\left(\frac{f_1 - e_1^d}{e_1^u - e_1^d}\right) + C_1^d e_1^d\left(\frac{e_1^u - f_1}{e_1^u - e_1^d}\right)\right\},$$ (8.36)

where we have used interest rate parity

$$f_1 = e_0\left(\frac{1 + r_b}{1 + r_f}\right).$$ (8.37)

Note that, after a suitable substitution, the above expression can be interpreted as follows:

$$C_0 = \left(\frac{1}{1 + r_b}\right)\{p^* \times C_1^u e_1^u + (1 - p^*) \times C_1^d e_1^d\},$$ (8.38)

where

$$p^* = \frac{f_1 - e_1^d}{e_1^u - e_1^d}$$ (8.39)

is the risk-neutral probability for pricing any option on the particular foreign currency.

Conceptually, the claim that we can price a currency option in a risk-neutral setting can be expressed as follows:

$$C_0 = \left(\frac{1}{1 + r_b}\right)E^*\left[\tilde{C}_1\right].$$ (8.40)

To continue with the numerical example above, we first determine the forward exchange rate at maturity of the currency option as follows:

$$f_1 = 1 \times \frac{100/80}{100/90}$$

$$= \frac{90}{80}$$

$$= \$1.125/\$.$$

Now we are ready to find the risk-neutral probability:

$$p^* = \frac{1.125 - 0.5}{2 - 0.5}$$

$$= \frac{0.625}{1.5}$$

$$= 0.4167.$$

Therefore, this currency option price today is equal to

$$C_0 = \left(\frac{1}{100/80} \right) (0.4167 \times 1 \times 2 + 0.5833 \times 0 \times 0.5)$$

$$= \$0.6667.$$

We can also find the replicating portfolio. To generate this currency option's payoffs, we need to buy $1.2 and borrow 0.0066 bonds (worth $0.5333 at time $t = 0$) at the home risk-free rate. In the up state at the maturity of the option, our $1.2 will have grown to $1.3333. We deliver the $1 payoff of the option which leaves us $0.3333 that is worth $0.6667. As it happens, this is exactly how much we have to pay in order to repay what we borrowed at home. Similarly, in the down state, we still have $1.3333 and have to make a payoff of $0 which leaves us $1.3333 that are now worth only $0.6667. Once again, this is exactly how much we need to pay back our home loan. Therefore, the value of the currency option today should be equal to the value of the replicating portfolio today, which is $1.2 \times \$1/\$ - \$0.5333 = \$0.6667$. This checks our calculation above.

8.5 Currency Option Put–Call Parity

Here is a simple currency option arbitrage argument that establishes currency option put–call parity. Suppose we denote the spot exchange rate as e_0, the next period spot exchange rate as e_1, the forward exchange rate as f_1, and the home and foreign risk-free interest rates as r_h and r_f, respectively. Let us investigate the payoffs of the following strategies:

1. Lend $1/(1+r_f)$ units of foreign currency at the foreign risk-free rate.
2. Buy 1 currency put option on 1 unit of foreign currency with an exercise price of X.
3. Borrow $X/(1+r_h)$ units of home currency at the home risk-free rate.
4. Sell one currency call option on 1 unit of foreign currency.

The payoffs at time t_1 depending on whether the currency options are in the money or out of the money are:

Security	$e_1 > X$	$e_1 < X$
Lending foreign currency	e_1	e_1
Long put payoff	0	$X - e_1$
Repaying home loan	$-X$	$-X$
Short call payoff	$X - e_1$	0
Net payoff	0	0

More generally then, if we denote the currency call option value today as Call_0 and the currency put option value today as Put_0, we have

$$\text{Call}_0 = \frac{e_0}{1+r_f} - \frac{X}{1+r_h} + \text{Put}_0. \tag{8.41}$$

Recalling interest rate parity allows us to connect the currency option values to the forward exchange rate as follows:

$$\text{Call}_0 = \frac{f_1 - X}{1+r_h} + \text{Put}_0. \tag{8.42}$$

The intuition for this result is that a long position in a currency call option is equivalent to a forward (or future) contract and a short position in a currency put option. The $f_1 - X$ term is discounted because the call and put premia are paid upfront (i.e., at time $t = 0$), whereas the forward (or future) contract payoffs as well as the options payoffs are received at maturity/expiration at time $t = 1$.

8.6   Pricing Currency Future Options

In this section, we will consider the pricing of foreign currency futures options. These securities effectively represent a plain vanilla call or put option on a foreign currency futures contract. Consider the following binomial tree models for the foreign currency contract and the foreign currency futures option:

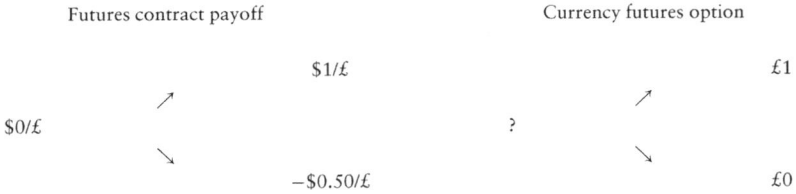

Futures contract payoff		Currency futures option	
	$1/£		£1
	↗		↗
$0/£		?	
	↘		↘
	−$0.50/£		£0

For completeness and for the purposes of building a replicating portfolio for the foreign currency futures option, we will need to model explicitly the home currency and foreign currency risk-free bonds:

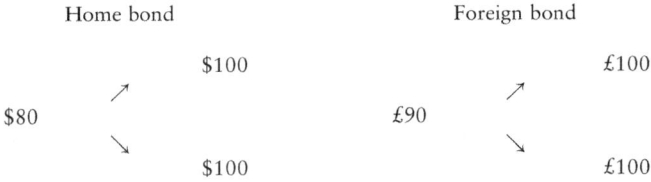

Home bond		Foreign bond	
	$100		£100
	↗		↗
$80		£90	
	↘		↘
	$100		£100

Let us construct a replicating portfolio using the futures contract payoff and the home risk-free bond. Let N_{fut} denote the number of futures contracts contained in the replicating portfolio and N_b denote the number of risk-free bonds in the replicating portfolio. We would like our replicating portfolio to have the same payoffs as the currency futures option itself or

$$CFO_1^u = N_{fut} \times CFP_1^u + N_b \times B_0(1 + r_h), \tag{8.43}$$

$$CFO_1^d = N_{fut} \times CFP_1^d + N_b \times B_0(1 + r_h), \tag{8.44}$$

where CFO_1^u and CFO_1^d denote the currency futures option payoffs in the up and down states of the world, respectively. Similarly, CFP_1^u and CFP_1^d denote the currency futures contract payoffs on both states of the world.

For the sake of simplicity, let us model the currency futures contract payoff as a fixed fraction, δ, of the current futures price at time $t = 0$. In other words, at time $t = 1$, the futures contract payoff is either a positive or a negative δ fraction of FP_0 or, algebraically, $\pm\delta \times FP_0$.

Now the above system of constraints on the replicating portfolio becomes

$$CFO_1^u = N_{fut} \times (\delta FP_0) + N_b \times B_0(1 + r_b), \tag{8.45}$$

$$CFO_1^d = N_{fut} \times (-\delta FP_0) + N_b \times B_0(1 + r_b). \tag{8.46}$$

The solution to the above system is given by

$$N_{fut} = \frac{CFO_1^u - CFO_1^d}{2\delta FP_0}, \tag{8.47}$$

$$N_b = \frac{1}{B_0}\left(\frac{1}{1 + r_b}\right)\left\{\frac{1}{2}CFO_1^u + \frac{1}{2}CFO_1^d\right\}. \tag{8.48}$$

Therefore, the value of the currency futures option at time $t = 0$ is equal to the value of the replicating portfolio at time $t = 0$, or:

$$CFO_0 = \left(\frac{1}{1 + r_b}\right)\left\{\frac{1}{2} \times CFO_1^u + \frac{1}{2} \times CFO_1^d\right\}. \tag{8.49}$$

8.7 Currency Futures Option Put–Call Parity

A currency futures call option upon maturity delivers a cash payment equal to the difference between the currency futures price at maturity of the option, $\tilde{FP}_1$, and a strike price, X, or zero if the option is out of the money. A currency futures put option upon maturity delivers a cash payment equal to the difference between the strike price, X, and the currency futures price at the maturity of the option, $\tilde{FP}_1$, or zero if the former is negative.

Consider the payoffs of the following strategies:

1. Go long in 1 currency futures contract.
2. Buy 1 currency futures put option with strike price X.
3. Sell 1 currency futures call option with strike price X.
4. Borrow $(X - FP_0)/(1 + r_b)$ units of home currency.

The payoffs from this strategy, depending on the currency futures price at the maturity of both options are as follows:

Security	$FP_1 > X$	$FP_1 < X$
Long currency futures contract	$FP_1 - FP_0$	$FP_1 - FP_0$
Long currency futures put	0	$X - FP_1$
Short currency futures call	$-(FP_1 - X)$	0
Repaying home currency loan	$-(X - FP_0)$	$-(X - FP_0)$
Net payoff	0	0

Therefore, a long currency futures put minus a short currency futures call is equivalent to risk-free borrowing in home currency and a long currency futures contract on the underlying foreign currency. Mathematically, we can express currency futures put–call option parity as follows:

$$\text{CFCall}_0 - \text{CFPut}_0 = \frac{FP_0 - X}{1 + r_h}, \tag{8.50}$$

where the difference between the currency futures price today and the strike price is discounted for the same reason as for currency options put–call parity, namely, because the premia are paid upfront whereas the currency futures and currency futures option payoffs take place at the maturity of the latter.

Problems

1. Why is the forward exchange rate, f_1, replacing the risk-free rate in the calculation of p^* in (8.39)?
2. In the currency future option pricing formula, we are discounting the expected currency futures option payoff with the home country's risk-free rate. Explain why.
3. Why is the foreign country's risk-free rate r_f missing in (8.49)?
4. You are asked to design a 180-day forward foreign exchange dollar contract for a Turkish bank. You are provided with the following information. The annualized borrowing rate on US dollars for 180-day term is $r_f^B = 6\%$ while the annualized lending rate on US dollars for 180-day term is $r_f^L = 4\%$. At the same time, the

annualized borrowing rate on YTL for 180-day term is $r_h^B = 20\%$ while the annualized lending rate on YTL for 180-day term is $r_h^l = 16\%$. The spot exchange rates are YTL 1.3410–1.3560/\$. What is the most competitive bid–ask quote for a 180-day forward exchange rate between US dollars and YTL?

9

What Next?

9.1 Contingent Convertible Securities

Consider the so-called "death spiral" convertible. This is an example of the contingent convertible (COCO) securities widely proposed as a potential solution for automatic equity recapitalization of troubled banks following the financial crisis of 2008.

Suppose that the assets of the firm are driven by a two-state binomial model and the risk-free rate of interest is equal to zero.

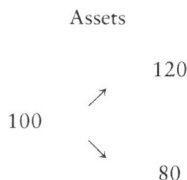

Assets

$$
100 \nearrow 120 \\
\searrow 80
$$

In this case, the asset return in the up state is equal to 0.2, or 20%, while the asset return in the down state is equal to -0.2, or -20%. As the risk-free rate is equal to 0, then it is straightforward to show that $p_u^* = 0.5$ and $p_d^* = 0.5$. The company has a zero-coupon COCO bond with one period to maturity and face value of 75. The bond is convertible into 11 shares of common stock at the maturity of the bond at the option of the bondholder in the up state and 19 shares of common stock in the down state. If we assume initially that there is no conversion, then the payoffs of the corporate bond are 75 in the up state and 75 in the down state. The value of the corporate bond today is

$$
\left(\frac{1}{1+0}\right)(0.5 \times 75 + 0.5 \times 75) = 75. \tag{9.1}
$$

The value of the share of common stock is simply equal to 25. The yield to maturity of the COCO bond is equal to 0% resulting in a default premium or a credit spread of 0%. Since the asset value is always more than the face value of this COCO bond, it is effectively risk-free if not converted into shares of common stock. However, optimal conversion may increase the value of the COCO bond to bondholders tremendously at the expense of diluting the share value of existing stockholders.

Consider next the case where bondholders convert their corporate bonds whenever it is beneficial to them. Note that in this case bondholders will always convert. In the up state, it is optimal for them to exercise the conversion option even in the face of a dilution of the value of equity. In this case, the payoffs to the convertible corporate bond are 110 in the up state and 76 in the down state as follows:

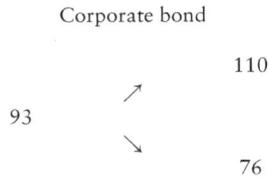

Corporate bond

$$
\begin{array}{ccc}
 & & 110 \\
 & \nearrow & \\
93 & & \\
 & \searrow & \\
 & & 76
\end{array}
$$

The value of the convertible corporate bond today is

$$\left(\frac{1}{1+0}\right)(0.5 \times 110 + 0.5 \times 76) = 93, \tag{9.2}$$

resulting in a promised yield to maturity equal to -1.32% and a default premium or a credit spread of -1.32%. This sounds like a very bizarre situation but happens occasionally to the quoted promised yield to maturity of convertible bonds when the stock price is too low and the conversion option is deep in the money.

The company also has equity outstanding the payoffs for which are given as follows:

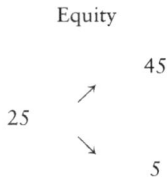

Equity

$$
\begin{array}{ccc}
 & & 45 \\
 & \nearrow & \\
25 & & \\
 & \searrow & \\
 & & 5
\end{array}
$$

The value of the equity today, assuming no conversion, is

$$\left(\frac{1}{1+0}\right)(0.5 \times 45 + 0.5 \times 5) = 25. \tag{9.3}$$

The value of the equity today with optimal conversion by the bondholders is

$$\left(\frac{1}{1+0}\right)(0.5 \times 10 + 0.5 \times 4) = 7. \tag{9.4}$$

Note that the sum of the values of equity and the convertible corporate bond (93+7) is exactly equal to the value of assets today (100). This incredible amount of dilution is not surprising given the generous conversion rates assumed. Existing shareholders effectively lose 72% as bondholders optimally choose to convert the COCO bond. This is the reason for the term "death spiral" convertible. In order to qualify for this ominous status, the convertible has to have a conversion ratio that increases as the underlying stock prices decrease.

In practice, recapitalizing troubled banks is, frequently, at the discretion of the bank regulator. For example, a few of the major commercial banks in Australia have recently issued COCO debt where the decision to trigger the conversion is solely at the discretion of the Reserve Bank of Australia (RBA). This is still untested territory and it is not quite clear what criteria will be used by the RBA if such an event were to occur in the future.

9.2 Longevity Swaps

Longevity risk is the risk that the members of a defined benefit pension fund will outlive the assets of the fund itself. This issue does not arise for defined contribution pension plans. The primary reason for longevity risk includes inappropriate assumptions about future rates of return, insufficient member contributions, and the secular increase in the life spans of a defined benefit plan members. The latter issue, in particular, has been the driving force behind the creation of longevity swaps which can be entered into by the pension fund in order to compensate the assets of the fund for any future decreases in mortality rates.

Lee and Carter (1992) propose a simple model of US mortality rates based on a large time series study of historical mortality rates by various cohorts. They also generate a sequence of long-term forecasts for future mortality rates well into the twenty-first century. Their model is usually the one that is used to simulate future changes in cohort and age mortality reference indexes for the purposes of longevity swaps. At inception, the present value of the fixed leg and the floating leg of the longevity swap is zero by construction. Over time, the net present value may be either positive or negative to either counterparty which gives rise to counterparty risk. The longevity swap rate is the rate that makes the fixed leg and the floating leg have the same present value.

9.3   Acts of God versus Acts of Man

In most of the stochastic modeling in finance, we take the state of the world as a purely random and exogenous variable which is independent of the individual or collective actions of the agents in the model. However, in practice there are few such random "Acts of God" type of events. In practice, in the vast majority of instances these seemingly random events are just the tipping point of mass of agents whose joint behavior leads to a break in a pattern of prices or trades.

The proper functioning of asset and securities markets depends crucially on a large number of market participants with heterogeneous beliefs, risk preferences, and various investment goals. Every time there is a critical mass of market participants whose beliefs and goals converge there is usually a large price swing. This can take the form of a bubble or a crash. The only way to stabilize asset markets is to wait patiently for the market participants heterogeneity to be restored in which case a crash is followed by a recovery or an asset bubble will lose steam and will be followed by lower more reasonable asset prices. These are the Acts of Man that tend to drive asset markets.

In terms of a policy recommendation for the proper functioning of asset markets in the sense of price discovery, the importance of promoting heterogeneous beliefs among market participants cannot be emphasized enough. Any feature or institution that leads to a convergence of beliefs will hurt this most important function of asset markets and lead to prices that can potentially deviate significantly from asset fundamentals.

Problems

1. Consider valuing a modified version of the convertible bond described in the chapter. Everything else is as given but now the

convertible bond can be converted into 19 shares of common stock in the up state of the world and 7 shares of common stock in the down state of the world. Compare the value of this version to the one in the chapter. Are you surprised by the difference? If yes, what is surprising about it?

Notes

Chapter 1

1. Strictly speaking, this equality is only approximate. Further conditions beyond the scope of this text are necessary to derive an exact APT relation. An alternative derivation is possible using a finite number of securities and a mean–variance spanning argument.

Chapter 2

1. Note again that the derivation of the formula for the present value of a growing perpetuity assumes $g_2 < r_{e,2}$. Applying the formula when $g_2 > r_{e,2}$ will produce a negative value which is meaningless. When the cash flows grow forever faster than we can discount them their present value is infinite.
2. Note again that the derivation of the formula for the present value of a growing perpetuity assumes $g_2 < \text{WACC}_2$. Applying the formula when $g_2 > \text{WACC}_2$ will produce a negative value which is meaningless. When the cash flows grow forever faster than we can discount them, their present value is infinite.

Chapter 3

1. But not from the denominator of the right-hand side. Note that WACC depends on the tax rate implicitly through the after-tax cost of debt.

Chapter 4

1. This unfortunate terminology has little to do with geography as there are European-style options traded in the United States as well as American-style options traded in Europe. To make matters worse, there is a third class of options that can be exercised at a set of prespecified times before they mature. Continuing with the illusory geographical metaphor, such options are, appropriately or not, referred to as Bermudan.

2. Another unfortunate term. Please do not confuse it with the concept of intrinsic asset value discussed in the context of DCF valuation models and intrinsic multiples presented in prior chapters.

3. Yet another unfortunate term. Please do not confuse it with the time value of money presented in Chapter 1. The time value of options is solely driven by the volatility of the underlying stock price and the time to maturity of the option. Another more mathematically intuitive way of thinking about option intrinsic value is to go back to the option maturity payoffs to the option buyer and realize that the convexity of the maturity payoff will push the expected present discounted value above piecewise linear payoff of the option.

4. Listed stock options on individual stocks have American-style execution but these options have 3 days remaining to maturity so for all intents and purposes they will behave as if they are European.

Chapter 8

1. Consider the difficulties of exporting a haircut.

Bibliography

Black, F., Derman, E. and Toy, W., 1990, "A One-Factor Model of Interest Rates and its Application to Treasury Bond Options," *Financial Analysts Journal* 46(1), pp. 33–39.

Black, F. and Karasinski, P., 1991, "Bond and Option Pricing When Short Rates Are Lognormal," *Financial Analysts Journal* 47(4), pp. 52–59.

Black, F. and Scholes, M., 1973, "The Pricing of Options and Corporate Liabilities," *Journal of Political Economy* 81(3), pp. 637–654.

Carhart, M. M., 1997, "On Persistence in Mutual Fund Performance," *Journal of Finance* 52(1), pp. 57–82.

Chen, N.-F., Roll, R. and Ross, S. A., 1988, "Economic Forces and the Stock Market," *Journal of Business* 59(3), pp. 383–403.

Cox, J. C., Ingersoll, J. E. and Ross, S. A., 1985, "A Theory of the Term Structure of Interest Rates," *Econometrica* 53(2), pp. 385–407.

Fama, E. F. and French, K. R., 1992, "The Cross-Section of Expected Stock Returns," *Journal of Finance* 47(2), pp. 427–465.

Heath, D., Jarrow, R. and Morton, A., 1990, "Bond Pricing and the Term Structure of Interst Rates: A Discrete Time Approximation," *Journal of Financial and Quantitative Analysis* 25(4), pp. 419–440.

Heath, D., Jarrow, R. and Morton, A., 1992, "Bond Pricing and the Term Structure of Interest Rates: A New Methodology for Contingent Claims Valuation," *Econometrica* 60(1), pp. 77–105.

Ho, T. S. Y. and Lee, S.-B., 1986, "Term Structure Movements and Pricing of Interest Rate Contingent Claims," *Journal of Finance* 41(5), pp. 1011–1029.

Hull, J. and White, A., 1990, "Pricing Interest-Rate Derivative Securities," *Review of Financial Studies* 3(4), pp. 573–592.

Jamshidian, F., 1989, "An Exact Bond Option Formula," *Journal of Finance* 44(1), pp. 205–209.

Lee, R. D. and Carter, L. R., 1992, "Modeling and Forecasting U.S. Mortality," *Journal of the American Statistical Association* 87(419), pp. 659–671.

Markowitz, H. M., 1952, "Portfolio Selection," *Journal of Finance* 7(1), pp. 77–91.

Modigliani, F. and Miller, M. H., 1958, "The Cost of Capital, Corporation Finance, and the Theory of Investment," *American Economic Review* 48(3), pp. 261–297.

Ross, S. A., 1976, "The Arbitrage Theory of Capital Asset Pricing," *Journal of Economic Theory* 13(3), pp. 341–360.

Sharpe, W. F., 1964, "Capital Asset Prices: A Theory of Market Equilibrium under Conditions of Risk," *Journal of Finance* 19(3), pp. 425–442.

Vasicek, O., 1977, "An Equilibrium Characterization of the Term Structure," *Journal of Financial Economics* 5(2), pp. 177–188.

Index

Lightning Source UK Ltd.
Milton Keynes UK
UKOW05n0910210916

283481UK00016B/317/P

9 781137 373021